THE U.S. ARMY, 1783–1811

CASEMATE | ILLUSTRATED

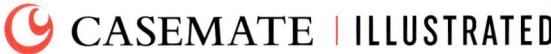

THE U.S. ARMY, 1783–1811

Defending a New Nation

John R. Maass

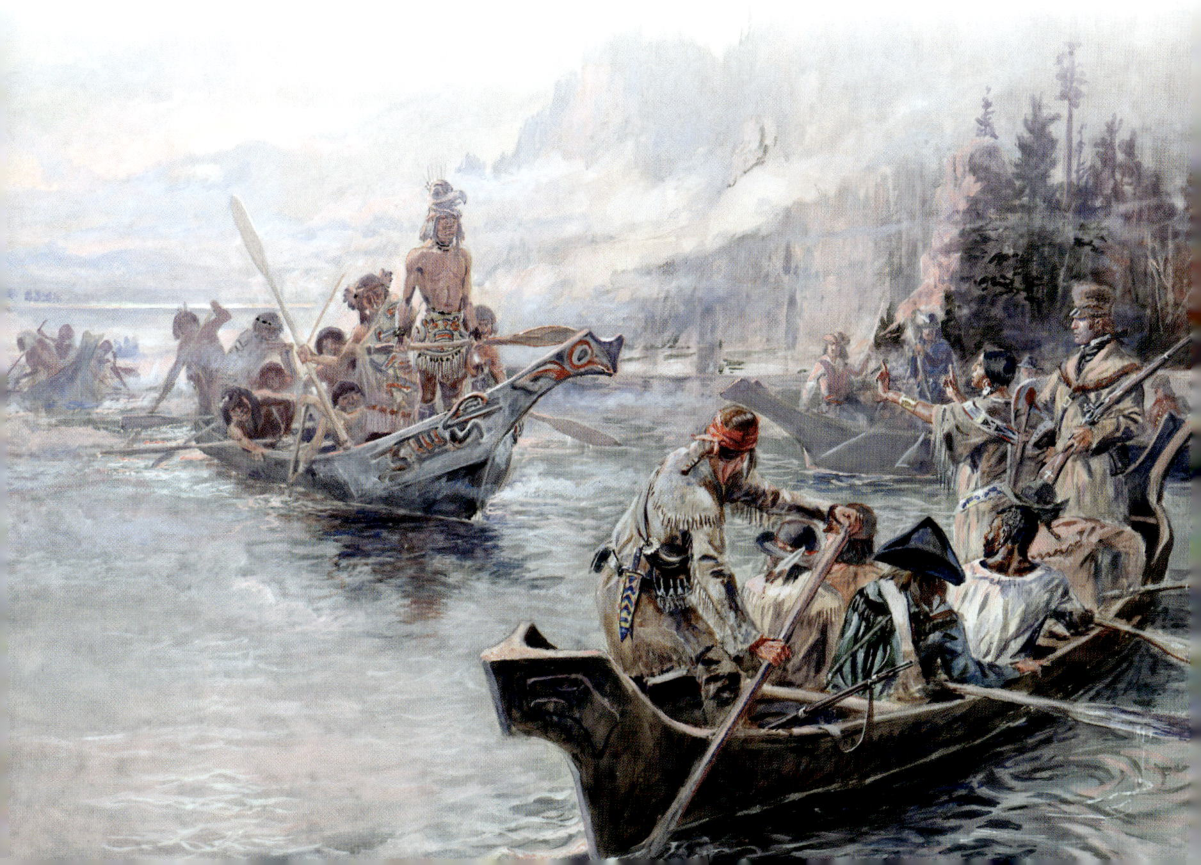

CIS0057

Published in 2025 by
CASEMATE PUBLISHERS
1950 Lawrence Road, Havertown, PA 19083, USA
and
47 Church Street, Barnsley, S70 2AS, UK

Main text, Center of Military History, United States Army, Washington, D.C., 2013
Boxed text and timeline by Chris McNab © Casemate Publishers 2025

Paperback edition: ISBN 978-1-63624-552-2
Digital edition: ISBN 978-1-63624-553-9

A CIP record for this book is available from the British Library.

All rights reserved. No part of this book may be reproduced or transmitted in any form or by any means, electronic or mechanical including photocopying, recording or by any information storage and retrieval system, without permission from the publisher in writing.

Maps by Myriam Bell
Design by Myriam Bell
Printed and bound in the United Kingdom by Short Run Press

For a complete list of Casemate titles, please contact:

CASEMATE PUBLISHERS (US)
Telephone (610) 853-9131
Fax (610) 853-9146
Email: casemate@casematepublishers.com
www.casematepublishers.com

CASEMATE PUBLISHERS (UK)
Telephone (0)1226 734350
Email: casemate@casemateuk.com
www.casemateuk.com

The Publisher's authorised representative in the EU for product safety is Authorised Rep Compliance Ltd., Ground Floor, 71 Lower Baggot Street, Dublin D02 P593, Ireland.
www.arccompliance.com

Contents

Timeline........................... 6

Building on Washington's Legacy, 1783–1790......................... 9

Securing the Frontier................. 21

The Whiskey Rebellion, 1794......... 44

Institutional Changes to Meet New Challenges, 1795–1800 46

The Army of the Early Jefferson Administration, 1801–1805 58

The Army and the Second Jefferson Administration, 1805–1809 71

Clouds on the Horizon, 1809–1812...... 79

On the Eve of War 92

Further Reading 93

Index 94

Timeline

From the closing days of the Revolutionary War in 1783 to the beginning of the War of 1812, the United States Army faced one of its most challenging periods. During this era, American soldiers confronted threats from Great Britain, France, and Spain. On the western frontier, hostile warriors from American Indian nations battled U.S. Army and militia troops north of the Ohio River, as white settlers' insatiable demands for land provoked conflict with Indian communities. The Army suppressed civil unrest, built roads, and conducted explorations, including the transcontinental expedition led by Army officers Meriwether Lewis and William Clark. The post-revolutionary years also saw the Army in a process of frequent reorganization, from the disbanding of the Continental Army at the end of the Revolutionary War to the establishment of Maj. Gen. Anthony Wayne's Legion of the United States, followed by President Thomas Jefferson's efforts at reforming the Army into a Republican institution. These structural changes increased during James Madison's first presidential term, as Americans prepared for war with Great Britain over maritime rights, free trade, and territorial expansion in a conflict that became known as the War of 1812.

Sep 3, 1783	The Treaty of Paris is signed, marking the official end to the Revolutionary War.
Sep 24, 1783	The Confederation Congress orders Washington to discharge the Continental Army, keeping only those troops he deemed necessary for the good of the service.
Nov 25, 1783	British forces evacuate New York City, removing the British military presence from the United States.
Jun 2, 1784	Congress disbands the last remaining infantry regiment and artillery battalion, retaining only 80 soldiers for garrison duties.
Apr 1785	Congress calls for 700 recruits for three-year terms of enlistment.

Oct 1786	Congress asks New Hampshire, Massachusetts, Rhode Island, Connecticut, Maryland, and Virginia to raise a force of 1,340 men for three years to put down the Shays' Rebellion in Massachusetts.
Jul 13, 1787	The Northwest Ordinance is passed, establishing governance for territories north of the Ohio River.
Aug 7, 1789	The Department of War is established under the executive branch to oversee the administration of the Army.
Sept–Nov 1790	Harmar's Expedition counters Native American resistance in the Ohio Territory.
Nov 4, 1791	St. Clair's Defeat, U.S. troops suffer about 1,000 casualties to an attack by a Native American confederacy.
1791–94	U.S. forces are used to suppress the "Whiskey Rebellion" in western Pennsylvania.
Mar 5, 1792	Congress gives the President authority to create a larger army.
Dec 27, 1792	The President directs the formation of the Legion of the United States, with an authorized strength of 5,190 men, to be organized into four sub-legions.
Aug 20, 1794	The battle of Fallen Timbers in northwestern Ohio ends organized Native American resistance in the Northwest.
Aug 3, 1795	The Treaty of Greenville is signed with the Indian confederation, headed by Miami chief Little Turtle, ceding most of Ohio and parts of future Indiana, Illinois and Michigan to U.S. control.
1796	The Legion of the United States is reduced to an authorized strength of 3,359 officers and men and renamed the U.S. Army.
1798–1800	The Quasi-War, an undeclared naval conflict between the United States and France, heightens U.S. military readiness and leads to an expansion of the U.S. Army.
Mar 1799	Congress authorizes the President to raise 30,000 more troops if war were declared or invasion seemed likely.
Mar 16, 1802	Congress authorizes the establishment of the U.S. Army Corps of Engineers as a separate and permanent branch, tasked with military and civilian engineering projects.

Nov 1, 1803	The Louisiana Purchase is completed, doubling the size of the United States and widening military responsibility to secure the new territory.
1804–06	The Lewis and Clark Expedition, led by commanders Meriwether Lewis and William Clark, maps significant parts of the North American West following the Louisiana Purchase.
Jun 22, 1807	The *Chesapeake–Leopard* Affair occurs, heightening tensions with Britain and leading to increased calls to enlarge the nation's military establishment.
Dec 22, 1807	The Embargo Act is passed. By early 1809, opposition to the act becomes so strong that Congress passes the "Force Bill," authorizing Jefferson to use the federal forces and state militias to enforce American commercial laws.
Nov 7, 1811	The battle of Tippecanoe is a major defeat for a Native American confederacy in Indiana, consolidating U.S. control over Indiana Territory.
Jan 1812	With war threatening, Congress votes to raise 25,000 new men for the Regular Army in 13 regiments of 2,000 men each. It also approves the creation of a volunteer force of 30,000 men.

Building on Washington's Legacy, 1783–1790

By early 1783, active campaigning by the British and Continental armies had ceased, and besides a small garrison of redcoats in New York, few enemy soldiers remained on U.S. soil. The American army, consisting of about seven thousand to eight thousand men, camped along the Hudson River at New Windsor, near Newburgh, New York, where General George Washington had moved them following the surrender of British troops at Yorktown, Virginia. Ill-clad, underfed, and rarely paid, the soldiers' morale was unsurprisingly low.

Word of a forthcoming peace settlement negotiated at Paris had reached the United States months before American and British representatives signed the treaty on September 3, 1783. With the anticipated withdrawal of enemy forces from America, the Confederation Congress on September 24, 1783 ordered Washington to discharge the Continental Army, keeping only those troops he deemed necessary for the good of the service. After the British evacuated New York City in November, Washington disbanded the Army except for one infantry regiment and a battalion of artillery, six hundred men in total, to guard military property at West Point, New York, and Fort Pitt, Pennsylvania.

Although most American leaders recognized the necessity for a postwar army, few agreed on the size and type of force best suited to the needs and ideals of the young nation. With the end of hostilities and the British evacuation of New York in November 1783, the key military question facing the United States was the kind of military establishment it required. Congress recognized that some troops were needed to counter Indian threats and to occupy America's western forts. Adequate armed forces would also be needed to guard arsenals and other important sites.

The U.S. Army, 1783–1811

Some congressmen, notably Elbridge T. Gerry of Massachusetts, objected to the creation of any standing army. He and others warned of the dangers and costs of a permanent army and preferred to rely on state militias to safeguard American independence and liberty. Professional armies and despotism went hand in hand, they argued, as ambitious or corrupt rulers could use an army to amass power and oppress the people. Other critics pointed to the several battlefield successes of militia forces during the Revolutionary War to demonstrate that American liberties could be defended by citizens in arms. More moderate political leaders argued instead that external threats and domestic disorders required a competent, regular

military establishment in order to survive. Among them was General Washington, who advised in 1783 that "a few [regular] Troops, under certain circumstances, are not only safe, but indisputably necessary."

As this debate was unfolding, three events occurred that gave credence to the arguments of those who opposed a standing army. The first occurred at the encampment around Newburgh, where many Continental officers were disgruntled. Having gone without pay for years, they feared that if Congress did not pay them or provide for their annuities they would face a bleak future of poverty. They had agreed in 1781 to a pension of half-pay for life, but as Congress grappled with a shortage of funds, the prospect for receiving any money seemed remote.

In December 1782, a delegation of these discontented officers delivered a petition to Congress in Philadelphia, demanding overdue pay and "a one-time lump-sum payment." The officers warned of a general mutiny against civilian authority if a satisfactory resolution to the financial issues did not emerge. Congress considered the petition in January 1783, but failed to act. In March, a group of officers called for a meeting of the Army's leaders, to consider threatening Congress with force to redress their grievances. Upon learning of the intrigues, Washington confronted the officers and urged them to remain loyal. Two weeks later, the arrival of news that a peace treaty had been negotiated in Paris reduced some of the tension, but the disturbing incident vexed many Confederation delegates in Philadelphia.

Shortly after Washington defused the crisis at Newburgh, numerous

◄ A scene from the siege of Charleston (1780), a six-week clash during the Revolutionary War that resulted in a heavy defeat for the Continental forces. (Thomas Mitchell [1735–1790]/Public Domain [PD])

Profile: Josiah Harmar (1753–1813)

Lieutenant Colonel Josiah Harmar was a formative figure in the history of the early U.S. Army. Born in Philadelphia, Pennsylvania, on November 10, 1753, he received a Quaker education before entering military service with a commission as a captain in the 1st Pennsylvania Battalion, in October 1775. The following year, he entered the Continental Army as a captain in the 3d Pennsylvania Regiment and during the 1770s he proved himself in a succession of command positions, ending the Revolutionary War in 1783 as a brevet colonel of the 1st Pennsylvania Regiment. He also demonstrated his capabilities as a military diplomat. In 1784, Harmar was appointed as lieutenant colonel commandant of the First American Regiment, and served as the senior officer of the United States Army from August 12, 1784 to March 4, 1791. Harmar was a brevetted brigadier general in 1787. Following his failed punitive expedition against the Miami Indian villages in 1790 (for which he was exonerated), Harmar retired in 1792, thereafter serving as adjutant general in Pennsylvania from 1793 to 1799, where he died on August 20, 1813.

◀ Josiah Harmar, by Raphaelle Peale. (U.S. Department of State)

Continental officers took a more subtle tack by forming the Society of the Cincinnati. Founded by General Henry Knox and other senior Army leaders in May 1783, the society was a fraternal organization, intended to preserve the bonds of shared wartime service and sacrifice, and to preserve the memory of the struggle for independence. The officer corps' desperate financial predicament and its pronounced feeling of resentment against Congress also formed a compelling impetus for the society's creation. Citing the sacrifices they had made while leading the Army to victory, the society's members advocated financial relief and postwar pensions for Continental officers. Some government officials came to regard the new organization as a dangerous political threat to the nascent American government. Moreover, the organization allowed for inclusion into the society of the eldest male children of officers who served during the Revolutionary War, with membership to pass to the "eldest male posterity." This provision appeared to many Americans as a conspiratorial threat to Republican principles for which the struggle for independence had been waged.

A final potential danger arose in June 1783, when several hundred unpaid Pennsylvania troops rioted in Philadelphia. They surrounded and threatened legislators meeting at the Pennsylvania state house, demanding to be paid. Although unharmed, the anxious delegates relocated to Princeton, New Jersey, without taking action to mollify the rebellious troops. The experience provided the delegates with a firsthand insight of the potential dangers of an irate army.

While these developments alarmed the Confederation government, Congress proceeded to study the matter of a future military establishment. In June 1783, a congressional committee led by Alexander Hamilton of New York and advised by George Washington recommended reliance on a trained force of professional soldiers to provide for the common defense, with the state militias playing an auxiliary role. By this time, however, sentiments within the Confederation government seemed to be leaning away from maintaining a permanent army, and the recent soldier riots in Pennsylvania did little to recommend it. Congress rejected the plan as being too expensive and complex. When Congress moved to Annapolis, Maryland, in November, efforts to provide for military defense ceased altogether. On June 2, 1784, Congress directed General Knox, the senior officer in the Army, to disband the last remaining infantry regiment and artillery battalion, except for eighty soldiers to guard military stores at West Point and Fort Pitt. No officers above the rank of captain were to be retained in the service. Nevertheless, congressmen recognized that some type of military establishment had to be fashioned to counter Britain's continued presence in North America and Indian threats against settlements in the Ohio Valley and Great Lakes area. Spain also appeared as a potential enemy in the South. Consequently, on June 3 Congress passed a measure to recruit eight new companies of infantry and two companies of artillery, seven hundred men in total, for one year's service. Congress asked Pennsylvania, Connecticut, New York, and New Jersey to provide the new troops from their militias. This force was not a national establishment of regulars dreaded by many congressmen, nor was it solely a militia or state formation. Josiah Harmar of Pennsylvania, a Revolutionary War veteran, received the appointment to command the hybrid force, known as the Regiment of Infantry, and later, as the First American Regiment, with the rank of lieutenant colonel commandant. He reported to both Congress and the state of Pennsylvania, and when Henry Knox resigned from the service later that year, Harmar became the senior officer in the Army. Recruitment for the unit was slow, so that by the early fall, only New Jersey and Pennsylvania had provided their quota of men. Harmar stationed these troops in northern New York and in the lands west of the Appalachian Mountains. Each of the small detachments was led by a junior officer, many of whom were Revolutionary War veterans.

The U.S. Army, 1783–1811

▲ A lively artwork depicts a debtor fighting with a government tax collector outside Springfield Court House during the fiscal insurrection that became known as Shays' Rebellion, which led to the deployment of more than 4,000 U.S. troops. (Wmpetro/CC BY-SA 4.0)

In April 1785, when the enlistments of the First American Regiment's soldiers were about to expire, Congress called for seven hundred recruits for three-year terms of enlistment. These new men were not to be detached from state militias but enlisted directly into national service, so that the regiment would be strictly a regular formation of the Confederation government. Congress directed that the regiment "show the flag" to the British still occupying forts in western territory ceded by Britain to America in the Treaty of Paris, and to protect settlers and American peace negotiators from Indian attacks on the northwestern frontiers. The troops were also expected to drive off white squatters from land in Indian country, destroying their homes and farms in the process, as some of this territory was intended by the Confederation government to reward Revolutionary veterans

Building on Washington's Legacy, 1783–1790

and to raise much-needed revenue through land sales. Despite these objectives, the regiment never effectively carried out its mission against Indians, squatters, or British troops, primarily due to its small size.

While frontier duties occupied the First American Regiment in the years following its formation, a disquieting event in the eastern United States came to have a profound effect on the American military establishment. Just as the Newburgh intrigues and the Philadelphia soldiers' riots alerted congressmen to the dangers of a standing army, a New England revolt led many American leaders to conclude

▶ A metal-working machine stands in the Springfield Armory National Historic Site. Established in Springfield, Massachusetts, in 1777, the factory was the first federal arsenal in the United States. (Victoria Stauffenberg/NPS)

The U.S. Army, 1783–1811

that a permanent force of regulars was required to guard against violent political unrest. The uprising, known as Shays' Rebellion, had a significant impact on the men who would meet in Philadelphia in 1787 to draft a new system of government, including its military institutions.

Shays' Rebellion was an armed uprising of Massachusetts backcountry farmers over debts, burdensome taxes, a lack of circulating currency, and oppressive court practices during the economic depression that followed the end of the Revolutionary War. Many of the rebels had served in the Revolution, including one of their leaders, Daniel Shays. They disrupted courts, assaulted lawyers and state officials, and threatened the national arsenal at Springfield. Local militia companies called up to disperse the rioters were often sympathetic to their fellow farmers' cause, and could not be relied upon to quell the disturbances. These chaotic events alarmed conservatives in all the states and frustrated those who looked for a swift, effective military response. Lacking troops, in late October 1786, Congress asked New Hampshire, Massachusetts, Rhode Island, Connecticut, Maryland, and Virginia to raise a force of 1,340 men for three years to put down the Massachusetts rebels, although the announced purpose for the mobilization was to send more troops to the frontier to thwart Indian hostilities. Only two companies of artillery were raised, but before any of these men could reach Massachusetts, local volunteers successfully defended the Springfield Arsenal from an attack in February 1787. The rebellion ended in defeat, but it demonstrated that the Confederation government could not act effectively to put down internal unrest.

While Massachusetts dispersed the rebels in early 1787, recruiting for the new congressional force was slow, so that by April, only 550 men had enlisted. With the rebellion quelled, Congress directed that the troops be dismissed, in part due to the expense of keeping them in the field. Only the soldiers in two artillery companies were retained to guard the Springfield Arsenal and West Point. In October 1787, Congress renewed the authorization for seven hundred men for the First American Regiment that had initially been made in 1785, and organized the troops into an infantry regiment of eight companies and an artillery battalion of four companies. These troops were intended to protect settlers and public land surveyors on the

▲ Patrick Henry (1736–1779) was a Founding Father and twice governor of Virginia. After the Revolutionary War, Henry grew resistant towards the growth of a strong centralized U.S. government, including in military matters. (New York Public Library/CC0 1.0 Dedication)

▶ This schematic artwork shows the U.S. federal defences around West Point on the Hudson River in 1780; Fort Putnam was constructed in 1778, the same year that work began on Fort Clinton (completed 1780). (Norman B. Leventhal Map & Education Center, Boston Public Library/CC BY 2.0)

Building on Washington's Legacy, 1783–1790

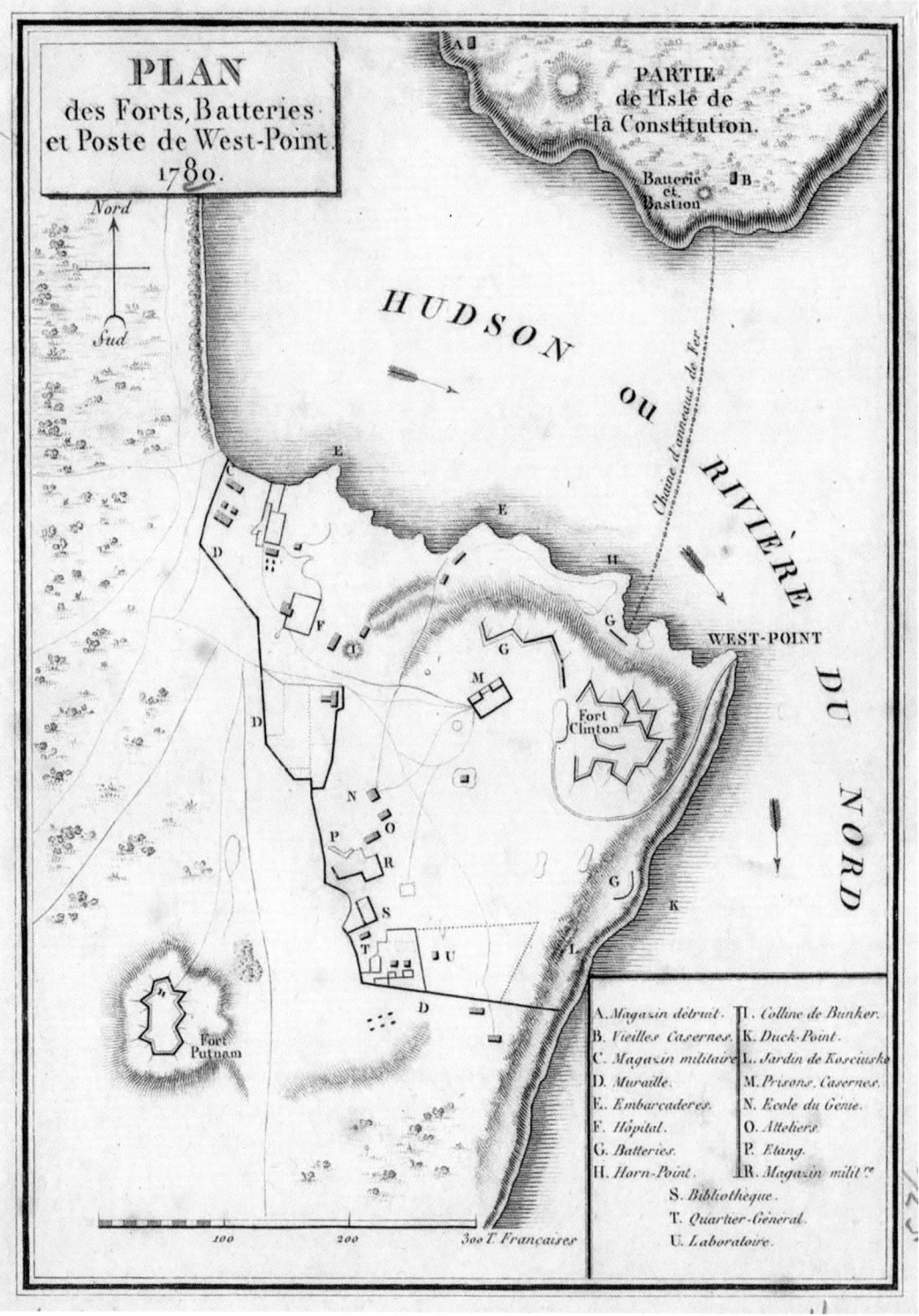

The U.S. Army, 1783–1811

U.S. Department of War

The U.S. Department of War (aka the War Department) was one of the administrative foundations of early American defense. It was created on August 7, 1789, and would oversee the operation, organization and maintenance of most of America's land forces (and in the 20th century its aviation units), until its dissolution by the National Security Act of 1947. The War Department was born from the complexities of attempting to control the Continental Army and revolutionary militias during the American War of Independence. At first, the war was run by multiple regional, siloed committees managing specific aspects of the conflict, such as supplies and recruitment. But on June 12, 1776, Congress sought to rationalize the situation by forming its own umbrella organization, the Board of War and Ordnance, run by five prominent members of Congress. It was an imperfect solution and in the post-war era a newly formed United States looked to improve the situation with its replacement, the War Department. This was signed into law by President George Washington on August 7, 1789 as a civilian-run, cabinet-level branch of government to administer the Army, Navy and Marine Corps, plus guide on issues of internal and international security, manage veteran affairs and keep relevant archives. The department was headed by Major General Henry Knox, who thereby became the first U.S. Secretary of War. The War Department had wavering first decades, being downsized in the early 19th century but then expanded and professionalized via focused sub-departments in the years leading to the War of 1812.

frontier from Indian attacks. At the same time, national and state political leaders began to reconsider not only the kind of military establishment needed, but also whether the government itself needed to be restructured. This movement eventually led to the meeting of the Constitutional Convention in May 1787.

Just as the Confederation government had struggled in the Revolution's wake with differing views about a standing army, so too did the delegates to the Constitutional Convention at Philadelphia. On this issue, the representatives were polarized along philosophical lines. Many who favored a new governmental structure—known as Federalists—argued in favor of a permanent force, denying that standing armies represented a threat to the public. They argued that an established regular force was needed to defend the country against a foreign invasion since militia troops could not be prepared in time to counter such a threat. They also pointed to the need to protect "against the ravages and depredations of the Indians."

On the other side of the debate, traditional Whig fears of standing armies, their costs, and the potential threat they posed to liberty were arrayed. To radical Whigs (later called Anti-Federalists), it was axiomatic that standing armies were dangerous to the liberties of the people, typical of monarchies and not republics. Patrick Henry of Virginia warned that "Congress by the power of taxation, by that of raising an army, and by their control of the militia, have sword in one hand and the purse in the other. Shall we be safe without either?" Others noted that the power given the new national government over the army was at the expense of the states, which only retained their prerogative in appointing militia officers. Congress, in the proposed Constitution, would have the power to raise an army even in peacetime, and could also control the state militia organizations. Although such concerns were heard frequently during the debates, the convention delegates did not seriously consider rejecting provisions for creating and maintaining a standing army within the framework of the new constitution. The Constitution was ratified on June 21, 1788 and replaced the Articles of Confederation.

Within the new constitutional system, the central government was responsible for raising and maintaining the Army, not the states, and the power to tax (previously denied to the Confederation government) meant that Congress could now do so. The Constitution gave the president the role of commander in chief, with the right to take command of the military in the field. Congress reserved for itself the power to declare war and to appropriate money for military spending. Army appropriations were limited to two years, so that the maintenance of a standing army could be reviewed—and controlled, if need be—by a watchful Congress. Congress could call out the states' militias to execute federal laws, to suppress insurrections, and to defend the country against foreign invasions. The national legislature also had the power to organize, arm, and discipline the states' militias, although as a compromise to federalism, the states retained the right to appoint officers and train the militias.

The initial army under the Constitution hardly seemed to pose a serious military threat to liberty. Congress authorized a strength of 840 men, but only 672 were actually in service, in addition to artillery detachments at Springfield and West Point. Harmar, a brigadier general since 1787, retained his command. Not until 1790 would Congress authorize an expansion, adding four infantry companies to the Army's authorized strength, which brought it to 1,273 officers and men, with soldiers to serve three-year enlistments. By early the next year, the force actually numbered eight hundred men, most of whom garrisoned several newly constructed western forts in the Ohio River Valley.

Meanwhile, in August 1789, Congress created the Department of War under the executive branch to oversee the administration of the nascent force. The secretary at war (soon changed to secretary of war) also assumed responsibility for supervising federal Indian affairs. Former Continental Army general Henry Knox led the new department, with only a handful of clerks and one messenger to assist with his routine duties. The administration of the Army included a civilian-controlled military supply system under the secretary of war, responsible for keeping and distributing supplies, while a board of the Treasury Department looked after procurement of military necessities, including uniforms and food. In 1794, Congress created the Office of the Purveyor of Public Supplies within the Treasury Department and a Superintendant of Military Stores, part of the War Department. Most of the procurement process was handled through a contract system for reasons of economy and efficiency, but this method failed to live up to congressional expectations or meet the soldiers' needs. For its weapons, the War Department maintained several armories and magazines for storing and repairing arms, many of which were left over from the Revolutionary War. Although Congress established national armories at Springfield, Massachusetts, and Harpers Ferry, Virginia, in the mid-1790s to produce and repair weapons, the Army relied on foreign suppliers for most of its armaments.

Most of the recruits who enlisted during the years following the American Revolution served on the frontier, in log forts built in the Ohio country. These were typically isolated posts, where the soldiers' duties were dull and laborious. Due to the logistical difficulties the Army and its contractors faced, and the challenges inherent in organizing and running a new organization, soldiers were often unpaid, poorly supplied, and ill-fed. Discipline was rigid and punishments severe, especially in light of the soldiers' frequent abuse of alcohol. In these conditions, morale was low and desertion rampant. Soldiers had a poor reputation among the general populace of America, particularly in places where posts were located. Many recruits were of foreign birth, primarily Irish, since native-born Americans were not usually drawn to the military's low pay. Given the costs associated with a permanent army and the small size of the force Congress authorized, frontier military operations also involved militia troops. It was with this mixed force of regulars and militiamen that the new government would confront the military challenges of the early 1790s.

Securing the Frontier

During the decades that followed the American independence, the new federal Army found itself confronted with an array of diverse challenges. Warfare with Native Americans in the trans-Appalachian West was the Army's first major concern, and it severely tested the new nation's ability to wage war successfully.

Challenges in the Northwest Territory

The lure of fertile lands, opportunities for land speculation, and the lucrative Indian trade drew thousands of Americans across the Appalachian Mountains after the American Revolution. Congress also had a financial interest in developing the West, both to reduce its wartime debt through land sales and to reward military

▶ *American Commissioners of the Preliminary Peace Agreement with Great Britain* was an unfinished artwork by Benjamin West depicting the United States delegation that negotiated the 1783 Treaty of Paris. While it shows the American representatives, the British delegation refused to be included, hence the void in the right of the artwork.
(U.S. Government/PD)

veterans for their past service. Establishing a buffer between the eastern states and the British and Spanish in the West also had the benefit of securing the territory for Congress. By the mid-1780s, a flood of settlers had entered the area north of the Ohio River to claim property, including many squatters who cared little for government titles or the Indians they displaced.

The Indian tribes looked on this encroachment with alarm. Although they had sided with Great Britain during the American Revolution, the Indians of the Ohio country were largely undefeated by the time of the Treaty of Paris in 1783. They naturally did not believe that they needed to surrender their territory to the new American nation—a sentiment the British openly encouraged. Not only did the British refuse to evacuate posts in land they had ceded to America in the Treaty of Paris, most notably at Detroit, Michilimackinac, and Niagara, but they supplied Indian warriors with weapons, ammunition, and supplies in order, Washington wrote, to "inflame the Indian mind, with a view to keep it at variance with these States, for the purpose of retarding our settlements to the Westward." The situation was ripe for conflict.

In response to settler demands and numerous reports of growing violence on the frontier, American authorities looked to the Army. Initially, the American government sought to restrain white settlers from occupying Indian lands, both to avoid hostilities and to permit the territory to be properly surveyed prior to sale. Secretary Knox prohibited the Army's senior officer, Lt. Col. Josiah Harmar, from engaging in offensive operations with his small command, which he moved in late 1784 to Fort McIntosh, Pennsylvania, on the north bank of the Ohio River. The Army thus tried to maintain peace along the frontier during the 1780s, although many military officers had little sympathy for the Indians. In addition to defending government surveyors as they marked off land in the Ohio wilderness, the Army evicted hundreds of squatters from land they illegally occupied. Beginning in 1785, Harmar sent troops to remove unlawful settlers, tear down their cabins, and destroy their crops. These draconian measures, executed in hopes of avoiding a war between whites and Indians, did little to endear the Army to western settlers. In order to increase the Army's military presence in the northwest and to keep an eye on Indians and settlers alike, soldiers built several log forts along the Ohio River and its tributaries in the mid-1780s. Ironically, the construction of these forts encouraged rather than deterred white settlement since the garrisons offered at least some protection from Indian attacks (Map 1).

Desirous of avoiding a full-scale war with the Indians in the northwest for which the Army was ill-prepared, the United States attempted to negotiate with native tribes in the 1780s. Government authorities reckoned that it was more advantageous and cheaper to purchase land from the Indians than to fight them. Despite these aims, most of these diplomatic efforts were unsuccessful. Attempts

Map 1

The U.S. Army, 1783–1811

at peace were doomed by the American position that the Indians had forfeited the lands of the Ohio country by their alliance with the British during the Revolutionary War. Negotiations went nowhere with the Indians, primarily the Miami, Shawnee, and Kickapoo, who refused to sell or trade away their lands and declined to recognize the legitimacy of prior treaties with the Americans. They insisted that the boundary between Indian and white territory was the Ohio River, despite treaties signed at Fort McIntosh in 1785 and Fort Finney in 1786, where Indians unauthorized to negotiate for all tribes relinquished tens of thousands of acres north of the river.

By 1786, backcountry warfare had broken out in the northwest between aggressive settlers and enraged Indians, especially those on the Wabash, Miami, and Maumee Rivers. There was much unity among the Indians of the Ohio country due to shared opposition to the encroaching Americans. Attacks on settlers and isolated detachments of American soldiers increased. In July 1788, for instance, Indians attacked a detachment of thirty troops near the mouth of the Wabash in a skirmish that left eight soldiers dead and ten wounded. That same month, a small party of soldiers preparing a treaty council site at the Falls of the Muskingum suffered an unexpected attack by a Chippewa war party and withdrew to Fort Harmar after the sharp skirmish. After significant violence between Indians and Kentucky militia forces, particularly in the Wabash River area around Fort Knox, a small contingent of regulars led by Maj. John F. Hamtramck occupied the old French settlement at Vincennes in 1787, to keep the peace and to establish civil authority in the region. There were, however, too few soldiers in Hamtramck's force to do more than watch the escalating violence. Much of the bloodshed stemmed from periodic raids north of the Ohio River launched by mounted Kentucky militiamen, who took matters into their own hands rather than rely on the small national Army.

▼ Two Native Americans ponder the scale and challenge of an American fortification in Ohio in this artwork from the early 20th century. Fortifications took anywhere from a few days to several months to construct, depending on the sophistication and scale of the structures. (New York Public Library)

In 1787, Congress passed the Northwest Ordinance to establish a workable process for governing these unruly territories. By August 1789, the first president of the United States of America under the Constitution, George Washington, determined that frontier violence required the "immediate intervention of the General Government," and in September Congress empowered him to call on state militia forces to help protect the frontier. Peace efforts during 1789 and 1790 by Arthur St. Clair, the first governor of the Northwest Territory, were unsuccessful, which led the former Revolutionary War general to advise Washington that a punitive expedition against the Indians would likely be needed. Under additional pressure from Harmar (since 1787, a brevet brigadier general), frightened settlers, land speculators, and militia authorities in Kentucky and Ohio, Secretary of War Knox ordered a foray against the hostile Indians on the upper Wabash in June 1790, to "extirpate, utterly, if possible," the Indian "banditti."

Harmar's Expedition, 1790

Governor St. Clair and General Harmar met in July 1790 at Fort Washington on the Ohio River (present site of Cincinnati) to plan the campaign. This post was garrisoned by seventy-five soldiers, soon to be joined by almost three hundred men of the First American Regiment. St. Clair and Harmar decided on a two-pronged advance against the Indian villages on the upper reaches of the Wabash and Maumee Rivers, the location of several hostile tribes unwilling to negotiate with American representatives. Harmar was to lead a march to Kekionga on the headwaters of the Maumee River, where over one thousand warriors were supposed to have gathered. Kekionga was a major fur-trading post, where British agents supplied Indians with muskets and ammunition. Harmar intended to destroy the enemy's villages, corn stocks, and Indian traders' supplies, to reduce the Indians to poverty, and prevent their continued war-making capabilities.

While General Harmar would lead the main thrust of the Army's campaign against Kekionga, a second force led by Major Hamtramck would provide a diversion farther west with a simultaneous march against the Indian towns via the Wabash River. Hamtramck, a former Continental Army officer, set out northward on September 30 from Fort Knox at Vincennes with about three hundred troops, of which only sixty were regulars, including several artillerymen and a brass 3-pounder cannon. The remainder of his command consisted of Kentucky militiamen of poor quality and low morale. Upon reaching Vermillion 11 days later, Hamtramck found the Indian village there evacuated. On October 14, Hamtramck returned to Vincennes due to the unwillingness of the disgruntled militia to proceed farther and to supply deficiencies. While Hamtramck's diversion may have drawn hundreds of enemy warriors away from Harmar's larger operation to the east, the Fort Knox soldiers accomplished little else during their brief foray and returned to their post on October 26.

The U.S. Army, 1783–1811

Meanwhile, Harmar organized the main thrust of the campaign from Fort Washington, from which he intended to march directly northward to reach the Maumee towns. Given the paucity of trained soldiers, Congress authorized calling militia and volunteers to increase Harmar's force. In the end, the 37-year-old general was able to gather approximately three hundred regulars and one thousand militiamen. The army also brought along two 6-pounder guns.

Securing the Frontier

At Fort Washington and during the campaign, the Army struggled with the two primary challenges that characterized all frontier operations during the era: logistical difficulties and undisciplined soldiery. Due to the vast distances from eastern supply sources and problems with military contractors, Harmar's forces were poorly fed, supplied, and equipped. The Army had difficulty procuring required munitions too, especially musket cartridges for the troops. Much of what did reach the posts on the Ohio River was of poor quality, or had been spoiled or damaged during water transportation to the frontier. A congressional report of 1792 noted "fatal mismanagements and neglects" in supplying Harmar's command, "particularly as to tents, knapsacks, camp kettles, cartridge boxes, packsaddles, etc., all of which were deficient in quantity and bad in quality." While supplies and provisions trickled into Fort Washington during the summer, militiamen began to arrive in September. About eight hundred men came from Kentucky, with an additional three hundred from Pennsylvania. Most of these troops were inadequately armed, and many had little or no experience with firearms or frontier campaigning. A number of these recruits were too old or infirm for the rigors of war, and some were young boys or paid substitutes with little desire to fight. Harmar despaired at the untested troops with which he had to conduct the campaign, but he had no time to train them before the army set off.

The militia, led by Col. John Hardin of Kentucky, began the northward advance on September 26, 1790. As they proceeded, they cleared a military road through the wilderness for the artillery and wagons. The regulars left Fort Washington on September 30, accompanied by the wagon trains, and by October 3 they joined the militia at Turkey Creek (near modern Xenia, Ohio). The combined force numbered 320 regulars and 1,133 militiamen. As the army moved toward the Maumee towns, scouts ranged on

◀ Fort Washington. (Library of Congress)

27

The U.S. Army, 1783–1811

the flanks and in the van of the column to guard against surprise, while militia units protected the rear. At night when the army camped, the troops cautiously formed a protective square for defense, with artillery, wagons, packhorses, cattle, and baggage positioned in the center. Initially there was little sign of enemy Indians, but by October 10 when the army reached the Big Miami River, scouts sensed that the column was being observed. On October 13, they approached within two days' march of the Miami towns and captured an Indian warrior who informed the Americans that the Indians intended to burn their towns and avoid the approaching American army. With this intelligence, Harmar ordered a mounted column to strike the Indians before they could escape. This detachment included six hundred Kentucky militiamen under Colonel Hardin, supported by fifty regulars led by Capt. David Ziegler. These horsemen set out the next morning, many of the men excited to finally strike a blow at the elusive enemy. The rest of the army followed in their path.

▲ Each infantryman would have a musket ball mold like this example. To make a new musket ball, he would melt lead or metal alloy in a crucible, pour the molten material into the mold, close the mold tight, and wait for the ball to cool in shape. Often, infantry would use their teeth to gnaw off excess material from the finished ball, sometimes resulting in lead poisoning. (Portable Antiquities Scheme (PAS)// The Trustees of the British Museum, CC BY-SA 4.0)

The intelligence garnered from the captured Indian was correct. About six hundred warriors had gathered at Kekionga under the leadership of chiefs Little Turtle of the Miamis and Blue Jacket of the Shawnees. After deciding they could not defend their villages against the approaching Americans, the warriors set fire to the towns on October 15, buried their supplies of corn nearby, and removed as much of their trade goods as possible. That same afternoon, Hardin's mounted detachment rode into Kekionga without opposition. The men plundered what structures had not been burned by the Indians, as well as those in other nearby villages. The main army arrived on October 17 and spent three days destroying cabins, crops, and stores. During this destruction, the militia became unruly, as they searched around the vicinity for additional caches of hidden Indian goods and provisions to loot. Harmar considered pushing on to other villages along the Wabash, but on the night of October 17, Indians drove off dozens of the army's packhorses, which placed Harmar's command in danger of being short of supplies.

On October 18, Harmar sent out a reconnaissance of three hundred militiamen and federal troops, "to make some discovery of the enemy" nearby. This detachment, commanded by Lt. Col. James Trotter of the Kentucky militia, planned to scout for three days, but soon after leaving camp, the militia soldiers killed two Indians, and later that day a few of Trotter's men encountered a force of fifty mounted warriors.

Securing the Frontier

With his militia unnerved by these encounters, Trotter returned to the main army camp with his detachment that day. His early return and his failure to secure much information about the Indians' whereabouts angered and annoyed both Hardin and Harmar. Hardin asked to lead a second reconnaissance himself the next day, to which Harmar assented.

Hardin set out with one hundred eighty militiamen early on the morning of October 19, heading northwest, accompanied by thirty regulars under Capt. John Armstrong, a veteran of the Revolutionary War. The militia was unenthusiastic about scouring the woods for the enemy, since the column expected to make contact with Indian warriors. Dozens of Hardin's men dropped out of the column to return to camp. As the Kentuckians found signs along the trail of what looked to be Indians in full retreat, Hardin ordered a rapid pursuit. In their haste, the militia became strung out along the trail and disorganized. Hardin and part of his force, including Armstrong's regulars, arrived at an open meadow near an Indian town on the Eel River. Once most of the militia was in the open, Indians fired from a half-moon formation in the surrounding woods, probably led by Little Turtle of the Miami. "When our troops were completely between the lines of the enemy they

▼ This artwork shows "A view of the Maumee [Miami] towns destroyed by General Harmar, October 1790." The Native Americans suffered c. 260 dead and 105 wounded during Harmar's campaign. (Ohio State Archaeological and Historical Society)

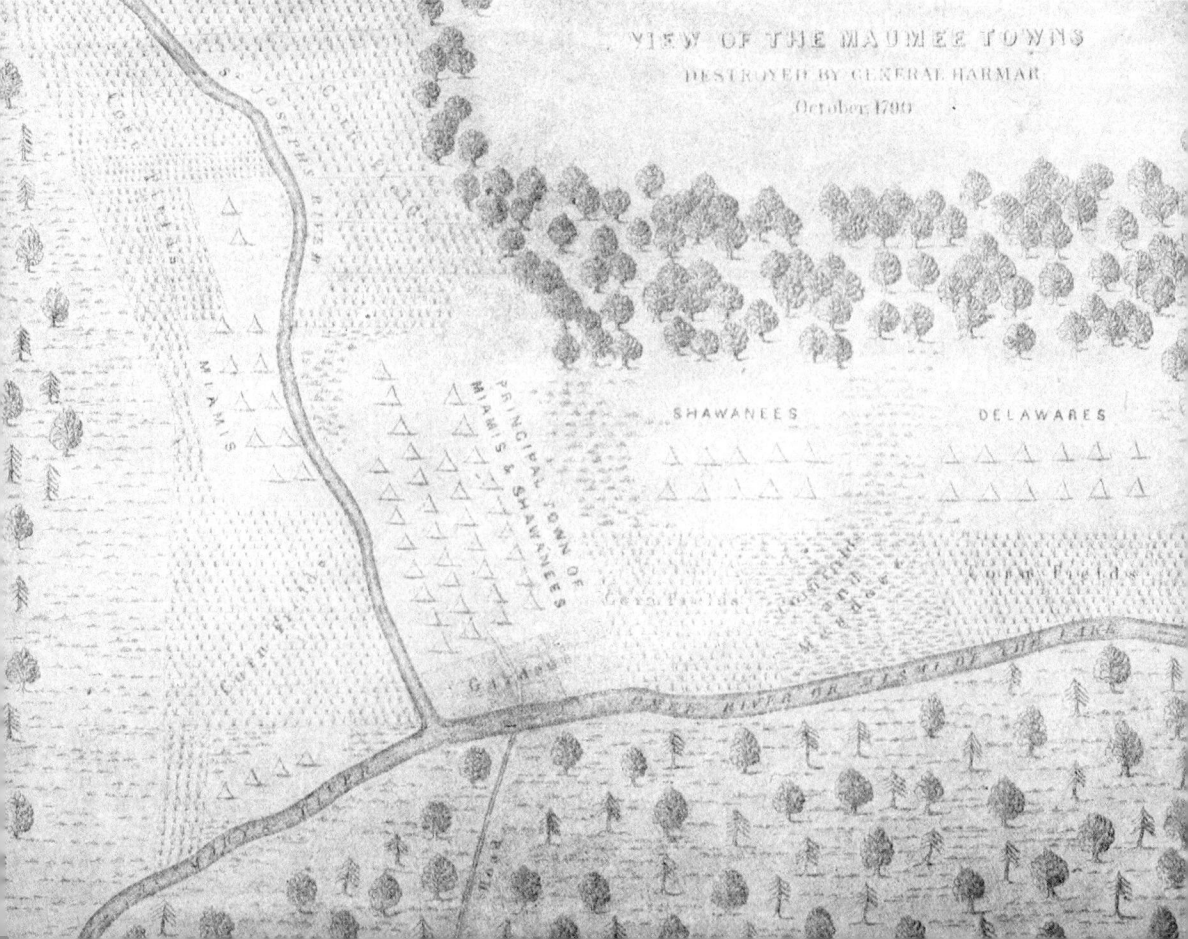

The U.S. Army, 1783–1811

commenced the fire with their usual yells," recorded a Kentuckian. Quickly routed, the militia ran in panic through the line of Captain Armstrong's regulars. Many Kentuckians threw down their loaded arms in their haste to escape, while the regulars stood and returned fire. After fierce fighting, Armstrong and another officer fled into a nearby swamp. "They fought and died hard," Armstrong later wrote of his doomed soldiers. Some militia did form a defensive line among the trees on the trail back to Harmar's encampment, which managed to stop the pursuing Indians. Meanwhile, Hardin and what remained of his terrified militia force reached Harmar's new camp near the Indian town of Chillicothe after sunset. One hundred militiamen were missing, along with the regulars, most of whom who had died in the clearing.

After the defeated troops made it back to camp, the rest of the militia became demoralized, and their officers feared a mutiny. Having achieved his primary objective, Harmar decided to return with his command back to Fort Washington. On October 20, his men razed Chillicothe and destroyed all the food his army could not consume or transport on their return march to the Ohio River. In order to restore discipline in his command, the general ordered that any signs of desertion, looting, or improper conduct on the trek back be dealt with severely.

While General Harmar made ready to return to Fort Washington with his command, Colonel Hardin wished for another opportunity to attack the Indians nearby, despite the setback of the nineteenth. Army scouts reported that over a hundred Indians had reoccupied several of the ruined villages of Kekionga to look for buried provisions. At the suggestion of Hardin, the general agreed to send a detachment back to the village and surprise these warriors, whom he assumed expected no further strikes from the Americans. A sudden assault on the Indians, Harmar reasoned, might also check attacks on his column as it marched back to the Ohio River. The expedition, the command of which Harmar

▲ Chief Little Turtle of the Miami Indian tribe was one of the most formidable Native American leaders in the American Northwest, a thorn in the side of the federal forces until his final defeat at Fallen Timbers in 1794. (Chicago History Museum/PD)

gave to an Army regular, Maj. John P. Wyllys, included sixty soldiers and about three hundred picked militiamen under Hardin. Wyllys and the militia officers planned to surround the Indians, and divided into three groups to affect the complicated scheme, to commence on the morning of October 22. Before the American troops could execute the plan, however, the Indians became aware of their presence by careless musket fire among the militia. A wild, confusing fight ensued, in which the regulars and the militia were unable to support each other for much of the battle. Indians attacked the regulars and some mounted troops as the soldiers crossed the shallow Maumee River in the morning. After a sharp fight there and at a second ford on the St. Joseph River, the Indians fled, although "the savages fought desperately," Harmar later reported. While the Indians suffered significant casualties during the battle, the American force had also been mauled, especially the regulars, who suffered approximately 80 percent casualties, including Major Wyllys, who was killed. The panic-stricken survivors, primarily militia, returned to Harmar's camp in disorder by the afternoon, having been "terribly cut up." Survivors reported that the fighting was "obstinate and many fell on both sides," including sixty-eight of the militia who were killed and another twenty-eight wounded. Word of the costly fighting alarmed the men back in Harmar's main camp, where the anxious troops continued to make preparations to leave.

Without attempting to bury the dead back at Kekionga, Harmar marched his dispirited men to Fort Washington, which they reached on November 3, their provisions nearly exhausted. Nevertheless, General Harmar considered the campaign to have been a success, due to the destruction of the Indian villages. "Our loss was heavy," Harmar reported to Henry Knox, "but the head of iniquity were broken up." He could also point to the fact that Indians never attacked or surprised his main column, nor had it suffered a catastrophic defeat. Others took a dimmer view of the campaign. Those on the frontier, in particular, concluded that the expedition had been a disaster. The regulars had lost 75 men killed out of 320 who began the march, and militia losses had been high as well. Others claimed that Harmar had risked too much in sending the militia on independent excursions, and that Harmar had never left the camp or faced enemy fire directly. Accusations flew between regulars and militia, and Harmar was accused of being a drunk. President Washington deplored the "disgraceful termination" to the campaign, which he called an "expence without honor or profit." Knox too called it "unsuccessful," and recommended that Harmar ask for a court of inquiry to clear his name in the face of such harsh criticism. Harmar complied, and a court of inquiry consequently convened in September 1791, at Fort Washington. The court exonerated Harmar, but he failed to retain the confidence of Washington or Knox. He resigned from the Army in January 1792.

The U.S. Army, 1783–1811

St. Clair's Defeat, 1791

The inconclusive nature of Harmar's 1790 autumn campaign all but guaranteed that a subsequent military effort to defeat the Indians in the Northwest Territory would be launched. In the months after Harmar's return to the Ohio River, Indian attacks on settlers and military outposts continued. In March 1791, the Washington administration appointed Arthur St. Clair, then serving as the governor of the Northwest Territory, to command the Army on the frontier, with the rank of major general, making him the Army's senior officer. Knox ordered St. Clair, an experienced veteran of both the French and Indian War and the Revolutionary War, to lead a force to the Kekionga villages and establish "a strong post and garrison" there, "for the purpose of awing and curbing the Indians in that quarter." A new fort would also disrupt British trade with the tribes as well. Until the campaign could be commenced, the United States tried a combination of diplomatic overtures and militia forays against the tribes, none of which were successful.

Despite the intentions of President Washington and Secretary Knox to muster a powerful army of regulars supplemented by short-term recruits and militia forces, St. Clair soon discovered that the army was "ill prepared in every respect to take the field." In the spring of 1791, St. Clair had gathered 299 regulars at Fort Washington, which left few soldiers to guard the other forts in the region. Even the men he had present were hastily recruited, with little training, discipline, or pay. In order to strengthen the frontier army, Congress authorized Secretary Knox to raise a second regiment of regulars to be commanded by Lt. Col. John Doughty, who had been on continuous military duty since 1775. An additional 2,000 six-month levies were to be raised for the campaign under federally appointed officers, all of whom would be discharged upon the conclusion of St. Clair's operations. The new general also had the authority to call out the militia of Virginia and Pennsylvania for federal service should he find it necessary for the success of his endeavors. By the time the campaign began in September 1791, St. Clair had approximately twenty-four hundred men, of which about eleven

▼ Arthur St. Clair, by Charles Willson Peale. (Independence National Historical Park, Philadelphia)

Profile:
Major General Henry Knox (1750–1806)

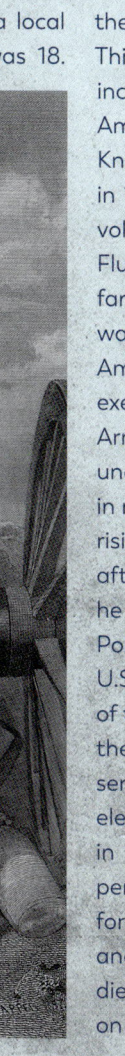
◀ A portrait of Henry Knox, suitably framed by a cannon (reflecting his position as chief artillery officer during the War of Independence) and holding a map of America. (Alonzo Chappell, PD)

Born on July 25, 1750 in Boston, Massachusetts, Henry Knox was one of 10 children. Knox developed two early passions: military affairs and books. He joined "The Train," a local artillery company, when he was 18. Two years later, in March 1770, Knox witnessed first-hand the Boston Massacre, even attempting to stop the impending clash by confronting the British captain Joseph Pierce. This event was just one of several incidents that hardened Knox as an American patriot. The following year, Knox opened a bookstore in Boston in 1771, stocked heavily with military volumes, and in 1774 he married Lucy Flucker, the daughter of a royalist family; together they fled Boston as war broke out. Knox's record in the American War of Independence was exemplary. He joined the Continental Army and served with distinction under George Washington, fighting in most major battles of the war and rising to the rank of major general after the siege of Yorktown. In 1783, he became both commander of West Point and commander in chief of the U.S. Army, also founding the Society of the Cincinnati. Knox resigned from the Army in 1784, but subsequently served in high political office, being elected secretary at war by Congress in 1785 and 1789; he was the first person to hold this office, and had a formative influence over its activities and direction. Knox retired in 1796 and died in Thomaston, Massachusetts on October 25, 1806.

The U.S. Army, 1783–1811

hundred were Kentucky militiamen. Most of the troops were on foot, as the general regarded mounted troops to be too expensive.

St. Clair encountered logistical difficulties like those faced by Harmar during the previous year. The distances involved in getting supplies to the theater and the inefficiencies of the Army's contract system created shortages of food, ammunition, muskets, camp equipage, and other necessities. Men in the ranks began to desert as discontent grew, and drunkenness among the recruits was a significant problem. Knox and Washington put enormous pressure on St. Clair to commence his movement, but "the means were inadequate," as St. Clair would later explain. Nevertheless, the commanding general appeared to be optimistic of success and began his move northward on September 17.

Cutting a road through the wilderness, the army reached the Miami River, where St. Clair built Fort Hamilton as a depot for the expedition and as protection for his lines of communications. After two weeks, the soldiers set out again, and ten days later St. Clair ordered the construction of a second stockade, Fort Jefferson, forty-five miles north of Fort Hamilton. By this time, the army was only thirty miles from the Indian villages, but with worsening weather, scanty food, and no pay, men continued to disappear from the ranks. On the last day of October, several dozen disgruntled Kentucky militiamen left the army in a body, with the claim that on their way to the Ohio River, they would pillage the army's supply wagons coming from Fort Hamilton. In response, St. Clair ordered three hundred regulars of the 1st Infantry Regiment to march south along the road to apprehend them and to ensure the safety of the supply convoy. This decision left the army deep in hostile country with few experienced soldiers, since the 2d Infantry Regiment of federal troops was

▼ This map depicts the encampment of American forces under Major General Arthur St. Clair on November 4, 1791 in the Northwest Territory. The surprise attack by the Native Americans resulted in a near 100-percent casualty rate amongst the Americans. (U.S. government/PD)

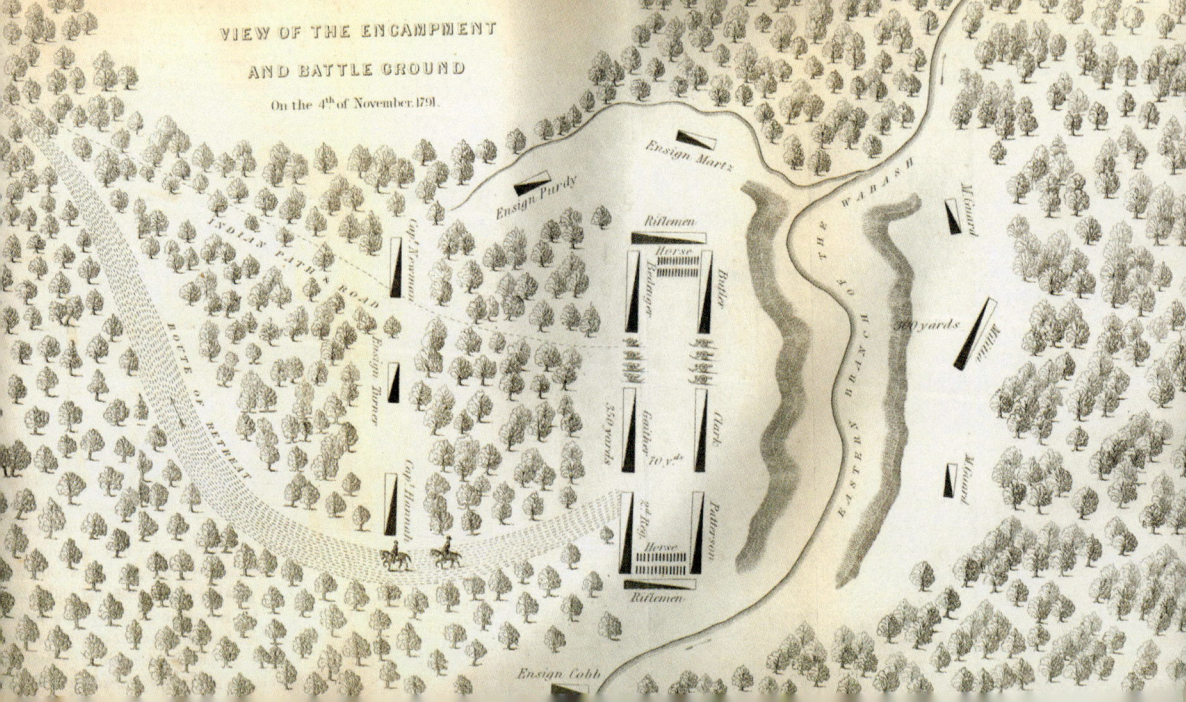

▲ This bucolic scene actually shows the site of Fort Jefferson in Ohio. The fortress was constructed during the Northwest Indian War under the direction of Arthur St. Clair, and served as a supply depot through several long sieges. (Nyttend/PD)

largely made up of recent recruits, "a great part of which had never been in the woods in their lives, and many had never fired a gun," St. Clair noted.

By November 3, the reduced column reached the Wabash River, where signs of Indians became more numerous, and stragglers were occasionally killed. That night, the weary main body camped on the eastern bluff of the Wabash River, while most of the Kentucky militia camped on a wide plain on the western bank, three hundred yards ahead of St. Clair's main force. Although alerted several times to the presence of the enemy nearby, St. Clair and his officers did not order the construction of any defenses, other than to have the army camp in a rectangular formation with the supply wagons and artillery inside it for protection. Sporadic firing by sentinels and reports of enemy scouts lurking about did not seem to alarm St. Clair and his lieutenants. Moreover, few security patrols operated around the army's perimeter to discern the location and strength of nearby Indian forces, which consisted of over one thousand warriors led by Blue Jacket of the Shawnees and Little Turtle of the Miamis.

Just before sunrise, shortly after the troops had been dismissed from their morning formations in preparation for continuing the army's movement, the militia on the west bank of the Wabash received a powerful attack from front and rear. Only a few of the Kentuckians fired their weapons before the bulk of them broke in "ignominious flight" toward St. Clair's main camp. The Indians attacked in a crescent formation, with the main part of their assault falling upon the left front of the American camp, once the militia took flight. Alerted by the shouts of the Indians in the forest, the American artillery opened fire on the attacking natives, but with little effect. The main camp on the east bank of the river quickly came under attack as well, resulting in great confusion and panic within St. Clair's ranks as enemy warriors surrounded them. Several units charged the Indians with their bayonets, including some regulars of the 2d Infantry, while others maintained enough order to fire volleys at their attackers. The fight around the artillery was desperate, as the Indians rushed up "to the very Mouths of our Cannon." As Lt. Col. William Darke of the Kentucky militia reported, "the artilery Men … [were] all Killd and Lying in heaps about the peases." Losses among the officers were particularly high, including the commander of the army's six-month men, Maj. Gen. Richard Butler, who, after receiving two bullet wounds, was tomahawked in the head and scalped while being treated by a surgeon.

After capturing the cannon, "the Indians got into our camp," a soldier noted, "and Scalped I supose a hundred men or more." Now convinced that the army's position was untenable, St. Clair ordered a retreat at about 0900. His command had almost been annihilated. A few officers managed to form a body of troops, break through the enemy encirclement, and gain the road. They began a retreat to Fort Jefferson, almost thirty miles away, while those wounded and cut off from the retiring column were left to a fate of certain death. St. Clair reported that the retreat was "in fact, a flight." The men threw away all that encumbered their precipitous withdrawal, including their muskets, and "the whole Army Ran together like a

◀ A picture from an article in the February 1896 issue of *Harper's New Monthly Magazine* shows hand-to-hand fighting between American troops and Native Americans during the battle of St. Clair's Defeat. (U.S. Army/PD)

mob at a fair." "The Indians ... tomahawked all that came within their reach," wrote one soldier. Most survivors reached Fort Jefferson on the evening of November 4, where they met the 1st Infantry. Due to overcrowding and lack of supplies at the small post, St. Clair decided to keep his column of survivors moving until they arrived at Fort Hamilton on the eighth.

The three-hour debacle on the Wabash was the worst military disaster ever suffered by American arms against a Native American enemy. About 55 percent of St. Clair's troops were casualties, with the dead and missing numbering 630 out of 1,400 men engaged. The 2d Infantry regiment lost three-quarters of its strength, and of the army's 124 officers involved in the November 4 battle, 69 were killed, wounded, or missing. Additionally, the expedition lost all of its artillery and most of its baggage, arms, and equipment in its headlong flight from the battleground. The Indians lost only thirty-five men at the battle. As a result of St. Clair's defeat, the American frontier became further exposed to Indian attacks, with the Army largely unable to prevent the depredations. St. Clair resigned his military commission in April 1792, although he continued to serve as governor of the Northwest Territory. A congressional inquiry in 1792 exonerated him for the expedition's failure.

The Legion of the United States and Fallen Timbers

News of the Wabash disaster reached President Washington and Congress in Philadelphia in December. Although these reports produced much consternation and political wrangling within the U.S. government, President Washington and Secretary Knox were able to put together a comprehensive strategy of peace feelers and military preparations beginning in early 1792. Negotiations with the Indians over the next few years proved unsuccessful, and Congress showed itself in no mood to make concessions. Additionally, the influence of Indian militants made compromise all but impossible on the Native American side. Meanwhile the federal government prepared a third military campaign north of the Ohio River.

The combined experience of Harmar and St. Clair's campaigns led to a reorganization of the Army in 1792, in which the U.S. government recognized both that it needed more troops and that the militia was unreliable. With the advice of Washington, Knox, and Revolutionary War veteran Baron Friedrich Wilhelm von Steuben, Congress created the Legion of the United States, with an authorized strength of 5,190 men, to be organized into four sub-legions. Each sub-legion included a troop of dragoons, a company of artillery, two battalions of infantry, and one battalion of riflemen. These sub-legions would be well suited for wilderness warfare against the Indians and could fight independently of each other. The costs projected for the maintenance of this force was over $1 million, a huge sum for the day. To command this new Army, Congress (at Washington's recommendation) appointed Maj. Gen. Anthony Wayne, a Revolutionary War hero known for his

The U.S. Army, 1783–1811

courage, audacity, and stern discipline. At the same time, Congress passed the first national law to regulate the militia.

General Wayne refused to be rushed into a campaign before his forces were prepared. He trained his men thoroughly, instituted rigorous discipline, and tried to build morale by his attention to the soldiers' clothing, rations, pay, and esprit de corps. In early 1793, Wayne moved his men to Fort Washington from their camps at Legionville, near Pittsburgh. For most of the year, he continued to train his troops, gather supplies, and begin construction of additional forts and roads north of Fort Washington as he awaited the outcome of ongoing diplomatic efforts with the Indians. Once diplomacy failed, Wayne was free to begin his campaign to extinguish the threat from hostile tribes along the Maumee River and its tributaries. Although he would experience logistical problems and difficulties associated with the militia as had Harmar and St. Clair, Wayne's command was in better shape than those of his predecessors. On October 7, 1793, Wayne led his regulars and militia forces northward to Fort Hamilton, and after a brief stay there, on to Fort Jefferson. During the march, the American army sent out numerous scouts and guards to prevent a surprise attack by Indians, but they encountered few enemy warriors along the way. By this time, Wayne began to face supply shortages and militia discontent, and hundreds of the Kentuckians deserted en masse. At the end of the month, Wayne decided to winter near Fort Jefferson and dismissed all the remaining militia until spring, in part to save from having to clothe and feed them. While encamped, the army constructed a permanent stockade called Fort Greenville. In March 1794, a small detachment of legionnaires completed a fort on the site of St. Clair's defeat, which Wayne named Fort Recovery, to signal that the area was no longer dominated by Indian forces. Wayne planned to proceed farther northward to the Indian towns on the Maumee, where the British were providing native warriors with arms and ammunition from nearby Fort Miamis.

▼ Major General "Mad Anthony" Wayne is here seen leading soldiers of the Legion of the United States in 1794. Wayne was a strict disciplinarian, but was also mindful of his soldiers' physical wellbeing. (U.S. Army Center of Military History/PD)

Profile:
Baron Friedrich Wilhelm von Steuben (1730–1794)

▼ Major General Friedrich Wilhelm Augustus, Baron von Steuben was one of the leading figures in the professionalization of American forces during the Revolutionary War. (Yale University Art Gallery/PD)

The life of Baron von Steuben was an extraordinary journey, from European commoner to American war hero. He was born into a military family of humble circumstances on September 17, 1730, in Magdeburg in the Kingdom of Prussia. In 1747 he joined the Prussian Army, then one of the most progressive military forces in the world, and from 1756 to 1763 he gained invaluable frontline command experience during the Seven Years' War. His was an eventful war—he was wounded twice and captured on the Eastern Front—but he also demonstrated an intelligent and organized approach to training and tactics. Furthermore, he learned general staff work while, from 1762, serving as aide-de-camp to none other than Frederick the Great. Steuben left the army in 1763, and served the next 11 years as court chamberlain of the kingdom of Hohenzollern-Hechingen. But in the mid-1770s, Steuben emigrated to America and joined the Continental Army. He quickly impressed Washington and was appointed a major general and the inspector general of the Continental Army. In the latter role, Steuben raised U.S. military professionalism, and helped develop the *Regulations for the Order and Discipline of the Troops of the United States*, a landmark training manual better known as the "Blue Book." After the end of hostilities, he was made a U.S. citizen and lived out the rest of his life in the northeastern United States, dying on November 28, 1794, on his estate near Rome, New York.

The U.S. Army, 1783–1811

The Legion moved out of Fort Greenville on July 28, 1794, with 2,169 men, accompanied by about 1,500 mounted Kentucky volunteers and over 100 Chickasaw and Choctaw scouts. The column advanced to the northeast after passing Fort Recovery, with scouts on all sides and the Kentuckians in the rear to guard communications. Determined to avoid St. Clair's mistakes, the army fortified its campsites each evening and sent out strong patrols to detect enemy parties. On August 1, the soldiers reached a major ford of the St. Marys River and halted briefly to erect two blockhouses surrounded by a stockade, which they named Fort Adams. From there, Wayne decided not to descend the St. Marys to reach the Maumee (which Harmar had done in 1790), but instead to follow the Auglaize River directly north to reach the Maumee at Grand Glaize, an Indian town Wayne deemed "the Grand Emporium of the hostile Indians of the West," which the Americans reached on August 8. This unanticipated movement confused the Indians and the British, and placed Wayne's forces between them. Here his troops built Fort Defiance, a major post with four blockhouses, to guard the army's rear as it marched down the Maumee toward Fort

▲ Anthony Wayne, by Peter Frederick Rothermel. (Philadelphia History Museum)

▼ The statue at the Fallen Timbers battlefield and Fort Miamis National Historic Site in Lucas County, Ohio, depicts (from left to right) a Native American, soldier, and frontiersman. (Victoria Stauffenberg/NPS)

▲ A mural depicting the 1794 battle of Fort Recovery illustrates how American fortress defenders fired their muskets through small apertures. Allied Native Americans provide them with guidance on tactics. (Canute/CC BY-SA 4.0)

Miamis. After a week of gathering food and supplies nearby, the army proceeded eastward on the Maumee's northern side, and on the eighteenth, began building a primitive stockade called Fort Deposit, where the troops left all excess baggage and supplies with a small guard prior to their final march toward Fort Miamis.

While Wayne's command marched from Fort Greenville to the Maumee, the Indians had collected a sizable force to contest the army's further progress. Approximately fifteen hundred Mingo, Delaware, Shawnee, Potawatomi, Ottawa, and Chippewa Indians under the leadership of Blue Jacket and Little Turtle waited upstream from Fort Miamis for Wayne to advance, with the intention of ambushing the army along the river. On August 20, many of the warriors took positions in an arc from the river through a section of forest blown down by a tornado years before, known as Fallen Timbers. Within the felled trees they met Wayne's advancing army. Since the Indian leaders were not expecting Wayne's attack that morning, only about five hundred warriors were in position when the battle commenced. An initial blast of Indian gunfire routed many of the Kentuckians at the head of the column, and seeing their early success, the warriors unwisely left the protection of the tangled forest and pursued the fleeing militia. Wayne brought up his regular infantry and ordered a bayonet charge against the Indian center after firing a well-directed volley into the swarming warriors. The troops performed "with spirit and promptitude," and drove the Indians from the protection of the timber. At the same time, mounted Kentuckians under Brig. Gen. Robert Todd attacked the Indian

41

The U.S. Army, 1783–1811

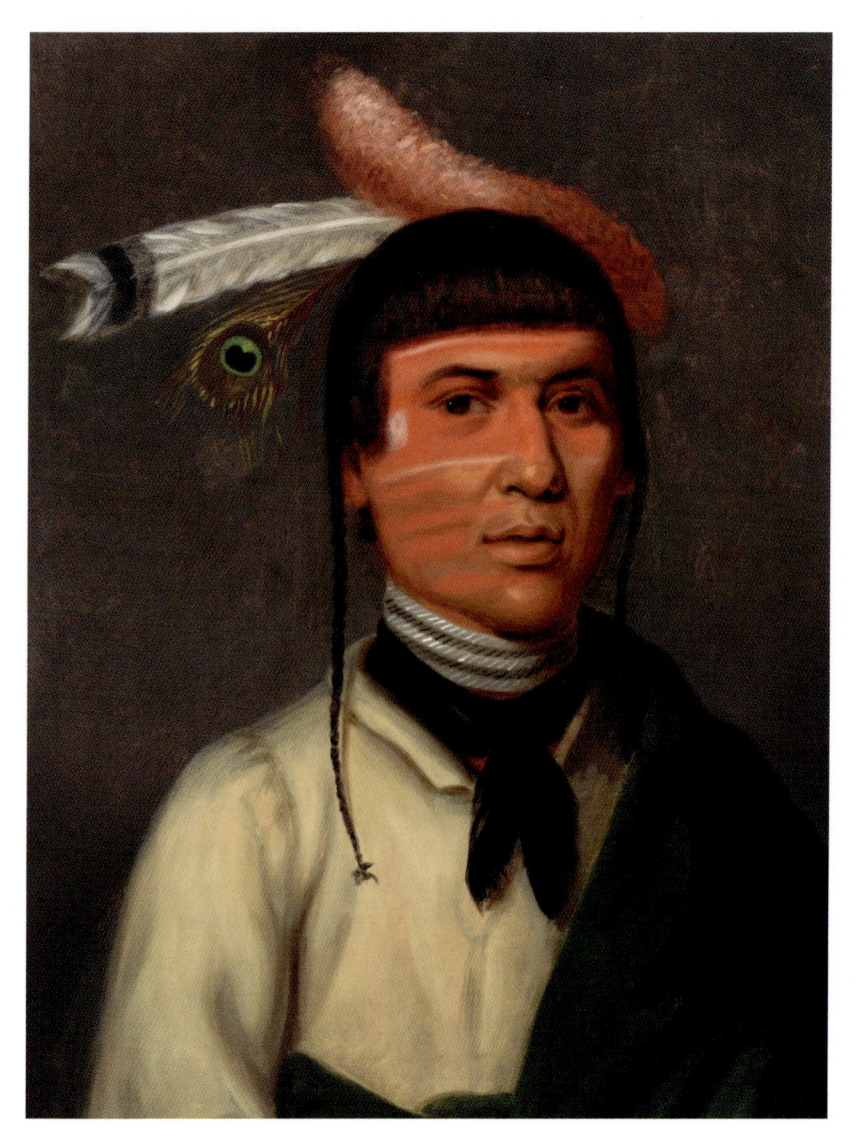

◀ This painting depicts No-Tin (Wind), a Chippewa chief. The Chippewa were a people of the American northwest, their territory originally wrapped crossing the northern plains and wrapped around the Great Lakes. (Henry Inman/www.lacma.org/PD)

right flank but could not cut off the warriors now fleeing that side of the field. The Legion's cavalry on the army's right flank made better progress against the enemy warriors in the open ground along the river, and put them to flight. Soon, all the warriors began streaming north for the protection of the British fort. The hour-long engagement produced relatively light casualties on both sides, although losses among the Indian leadership were particularly high. More importantly, the defeat ended the Indians' cohesiveness and will to continue the war, and when the British at Fort Miamis refused to come to their aid as they fled the battleground, the Indians recognized that they no longer had an ally. The Legion proceeded to destroy the nearby crops and Indian towns with impunity.

Securing the Frontier

This painting depicts General Anthony Wayne and Chief Little Turtle of the Miami tribe engaged in negotiations that led to the Treaty of Greenville in 1795, following the defeat of Native American tribes in the Northwest Territory. (PD)

The army returned to Fort Defiance a few days after the battle. The troops continued to destroy Indian crops and towns along their way while enduring sporadic attacks. In mid-September, Wayne moved to the Miami villages at the head of the Maumee and St. Marys rivers. Here the troops constructed Fort Wayne, in the heart of hostile country, left it garrisoned by one sub-legion, and marched for Fort Greenville, where the army arrived on November 2. At this post in August 1795, a coalition of Indian tribes met with General Wayne "to put an end to a destructive war, to settle all controversies, and to restore harmony and a friendly intercourse between the said United States, and Indian tribes." Having endured the devastation of the Maumee Valley after Fallen Timbers, the tribes could no longer wage war, or even survive. Instead, they agreed to a treaty in which they gave up land that would be admitted to the Union in 1803 as the state of Ohio, along with sixteen other strategic tracts in the Northwest. After five years of bloody war, the Indian conflict in the Northwest was effectively over.

The Whiskey Rebellion, 1794

Securing the Northwest Territories was the bloodiest, but not the only challenge confronting the young United States government in the 1790s. Besides the wilderness campaigns north of the Ohio River, the Washington administration faced a large-scale domestic protest movement in the backcountry of Pennsylvania, Maryland, Ohio, Virginia, and the Carolinas.

▼ This artwork depicting combat on the banks of the Maumee River in Ohio, August 1794, shows the typical uniforms of American soldiers and militia fighters around this time. (U.S. Army Center of Military History)

The movement stemmed from opposition to an excise tax on liquor and stills enacted by Congress in 1791. The frontier "rebellion" reached its peak in 1794, principally in the counties of western Pennsylvania, where protests and violence

◀ A painting by Frederick Kemmelmeyer depicts George Washington and his troops near Fort Cumberland, Maryland, as they prepare to march to suppress the so-called "Whiskey Rebellion" insurgency in western Pennsylvania in 1791. (Metropolitan Museum of Art/PD)

against tax collectors received widespread support. It became clear to Washington and his principal adviser in this matter, Treasury Secretary Alexander Hamilton, that only a federal military response could put down the unrest, enforce the tax laws, and demonstrate the authority of the new national government. The use of federal troops, however, was problematic in that the state militias had the responsibility to suppress rebellions. Moreover, most of the Army's regulars were serving in Wayne's campaign in the Northwest, and therefore unavailable. More importantly, Washington was reluctant to use the Army against rebellious civilians, even those under arms. "The employing of regular troops," the president wrote, must "be avoided if it be possible to effect order without their aid; otherwise there would be a cry at once, 'the Cat is let out; we now see for what purpose an Army was raised.'" Instead, the federal government resorted to the mobilization of state militias to suppress the uprising and "to cause the laws to be executed." Knox called on Pennsylvania, New Jersey, Virginia, and Maryland to provide a total of 15,450 militiamen, a huge number of men considering the size of the Regular Army at the time and the disorganized nature of the rioters. After marching to the Pittsburgh area, this force quieted the turmoil with little bloodshed. President Washington took personal command of the troops and marched with them as far as western Maryland. Although some of Washington's advisers suggested the use of a contingent of regulars on the expedition, only militia soldiers saw active service during the campaign.

Institutional Changes to Meet New Challenges, 1795–1800

The government's success against Ohio Indians and backcountry malcontents resolved some of the new nation's vulnerabilities, but others remained to be addressed. During the last five years of the eighteenth century, the Washington administration strove to meet challenges posed by an old foe—Great Britain—and a new one, France. In so doing, it had to wrestle with how best to provide for the common defense, always a contentious matter given the economic, political, and ideological ramifications of this question.

Building Forts and Disbanding the Legion

General Wayne's triumph at Fallen Timbers may have eclipsed Britain's influence over the American Northwest, but U.S. leaders understood that the British Royal Navy—the premier nautical power of the age—was more than capable of harming American ports and maritime commerce should the two nations ever come to blows. The deployment of almost all the Army's soldiers on the western frontier made it obvious that additional troops would be needed for the defense of the country's numerous coastal and riverine cities. In 1794, Congress began a coastal defense program by starting the construction of twenty-four forts, and adding over seven hundred soldiers to the Army's Corps of Artillerists and Engineers to garrison them. Soldiers manned forts from Portland, Maine, to Savannah, Georgia, typically in companies of seventeen or twenty-four privates, led by a captain or lieutenant and several noncommissioned officers. Additionally, the following year Congress authorized the recruitment of the Legion of the United States, still stationed on the frontier, to its full authorized strength.

By August 1795, however, the threat of war with Great Britain had declined precipitously. General Wayne concluded the Treaty of Greenville with the hostile northwestern Indian confederation that month, while Congress ratified a treaty "of amity, commerce, and navigation" with Great Britain, negotiated by Chief Justice John Jay, that settled many disputes remaining from the Revolutionary War. Although these two treaties seemed to promise peace for the new nation, Federalists still sought to keep the Army at its present size, since dozens of western posts soon to be evacuated by British forces in accordance with the new treaty required adequate garrisons. Moreover, the possibility of renewed Indian hostilities could not be ignored, especially in the Southwest. The Republicans in Congress viewed the military question differently, and a heated political battle ensued between the two factions over the size, composition, and anticipated

U.S. Army Fortifications

Military fortifications proliferated throughout the newborn United States during the late 17th and early 18th centuries. They embodied a range of purposes: enforce control over important trade routes (especially navigable rivers); defend vulnerable coastlines; act as expeditionary bases; consolidate new frontiers; overwatch American settlements. In terms of their construction, stone-built fortresses tended to be more common in the southern United States, where stone (or adobe brick) were accessible building materials in arid areas. Across much of northwest, central and northern Americas, however, the bulk of forts were made using timber, of which there was an almost inexhaustible supply in virgin forests. A common characteristic of such forts was an outer palisade made from heavy and tall vertical timbers, often earth-packed to improve resistance to missile attacks. Ditches and other earthworks provided further obstacles to assault. The palisade encircled a variety of inner buildings, such as living quarters, stores, stables and magazines. Fortifications constructed in more established locations, with significant local populations or strategic significance, tended to be more substantial in construction and more sophisticated in layout, even applying the geometric principles of layout developed by the French military engineer Vauban. Frontier forts, by contrast, leaned towards boxy simplicity. They often included blockhouses: square, solid two-story strongpoints designed to protect the fortress gate and act as a refuge if the palisade was breached. Blockhouses were also built in isolation, as positions from which a few dozen people could operate over the local area.

costs of the force. Most Republicans saw little need to spend money on a large military establishment when war seemed unlikely. They objected to the War Department's budget, which amounted to almost 40 percent of all government expenditures by the mid-1790s. Matching their concern over cost was their traditional antipathy for standing armies, which they feared could become instruments of oppression in the hands of their political opponents.

Although both General Wayne and Secretary of War James McHenry opposed any reduction of the force, in early 1796 after much legislative wrangling, Congress reduced and recast the Legion as the United States Army. Since cessation of hostilities with the Indians meant a change in the Army's role from an active campaign force to one better suited to border defense, each sub-legion reverted to becoming a traditional infantry regiment along the lines of the Continental Army during the Revolutionary War. The reorganized Army had a new authorized strength of 3,359 officers and men, grouped in four regiments of infantry, two companies of cavalry, and in the existing Corps of Artillerists and Engineers. In March 1797, Congress again revised the Army's structure by stipulating that

▲ Fort King George in McIntosh County, Georgia, provides an extant historic example of blockhouse-type fortification construction. Note the overhanging upper floor; the defenders upstairs could fire down on close attackers through apertures around the edge of the floor. (Bubba73 [Jud McCranie]/CC BY SA .30)

▼ Secretary of War James McHenry, by H. Pollock. (U.S. Army Art Collection)

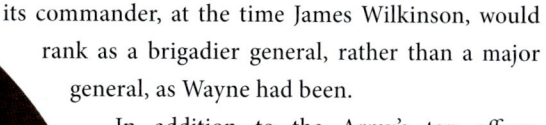

its commander, at the time James Wilkinson, would rank as a brigadier general, rather than a major general, as Wayne had been.

In addition to the Army's top officer, Congress authorized a staff consisting of a quartermaster general, paymaster general, judge advocate, brigade major, and brigade inspector, although the duties and responsibilities of the two brigade-level positions were not well defined.

By 1797, many of the Army's troops were located on the southwestern frontier, while other units remained posted in the old Northwest, particularly at Detroit and along the Canadian border. Most units were understrength, and many soldiers suffered from illness, poor nutrition, and lack of proper medical treatment. The Army's inadequate supply system

◀ James Wilkinson, by Charles Willson Peale. (Independence National Historical Park, Philadelphia)

Brown Bess and Charleville Muskets

In the earliest years of the U.S. Army, the infantry were largely equipped with the firearms of the Revolutionary War. In terms of standard smoothbore musket, these were principally the British Short Land Service Musket, Caliber .75—aka the "Brown Bess"—and the French Infantry Musket, Model of 1763, Caliber .69, or "Charleville Musket" (named after the French arsenal most associated with its production). Arguments about which weapon was best tend to lean marginally towards the French model, on account of its slightly more accurate shooting characteristics and its ease of maintenance, but both were reliable and effective types. Being smoothbores designed for volley fire, the effective range of the muskets was about 50–70 yards. For greater reach, marksmen used varieties of rifled weapon known generically as "Kentucky" or "Pennsylvania" rifles, based on German hunting models but progressively modified for military use. With these weapons, effective range was about 100 yards, but could be triple that distance in talented hands.

A MAP
OF THE
United States
Exhibiting Post Roads & Distances
BY
Abraham Bradley Jun.r
The first Sheet comprehending the
Nine Northern States, with parts of Virginia
and the Territory North of Ohio.
LAKE SUPERIOR
LAKE MICHIGAN
LAKE HURON
LAKE ONTARIO
ERIE LAKE
NORTH WESTERN
WESTERN MIDDLE EASTERN
TERRITORY
TERRITORY NORTH OF OHIO
PENNSYLVANIA
VIRGINIA
KENTUCKY
MERO DISTRICT
TENNASSEE
NORTH CAROLINA
SOUTH CAROLINA
GEORGIA
LAND CLAIMED BY THE UNITED STATES
CHICKESAWS
CHOCTAWS
CHEROKEES
UPPER CREEKS
LOWER CREEKS
SEMINOLES
WEST FLORIDA
EAST FLORIDA
APPALACHEE BAY
MISSISSIPPI RIVER
OHIO RIVER
CUMBERLAND RIVER
TENNASSEE RIVER
GULPH OF MEXICO
MOUTHS of the MISSISSIPPI
Map
of the
United Sta
Exhibiting the
POST-ROADS, the situations, connections & distances
Stage Roads, Counties, Ports of En
Delivery for Foreign Vessels, and the Prin
BY
Abraham Bradley ju

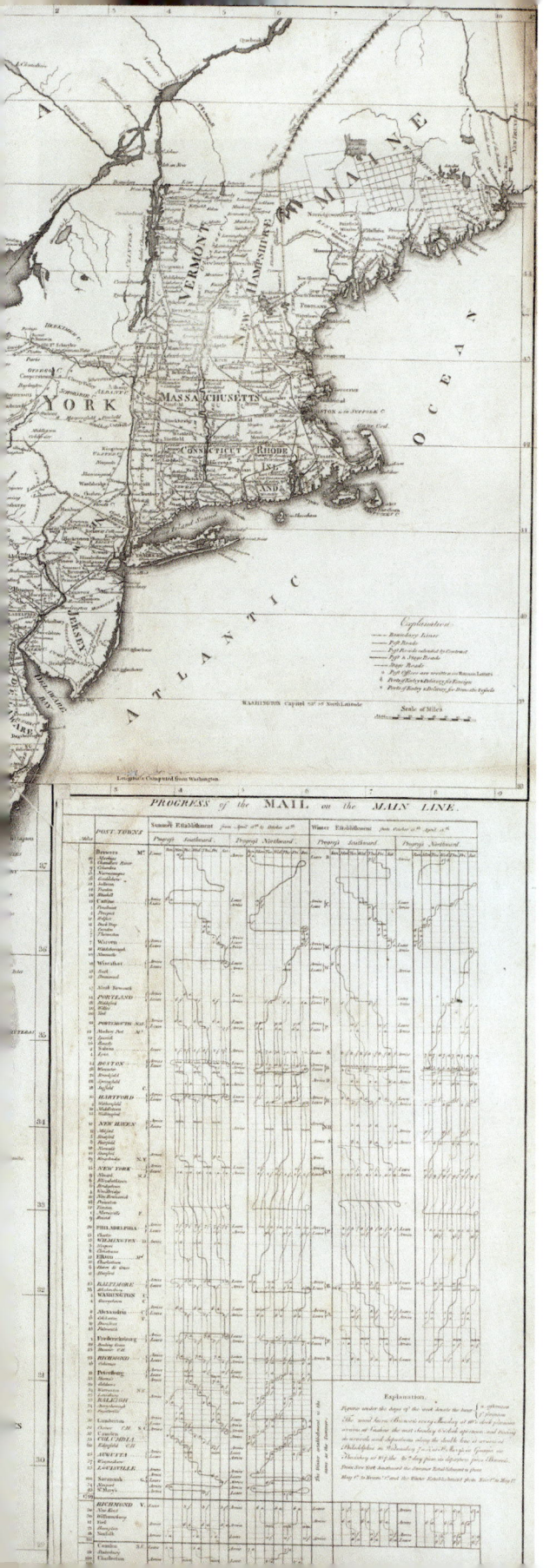

contributed to the troops' low morale and ill health, and the men received their meager pay infrequently. These chronic logistical problems were never adequately surmounted.

Mobilization for Quasi-War

Although the United States preferred to stay out of the escalating conflict between the traditional monarchies of Europe and the revolutionary, anti-monarchist government that gained control of France in the late 1780s and early 1790s, the nation found such a course difficult to navigate. By 1793, revolutionary France and monarchist Britain were at war with each other, but united in their antipathy toward American neutrality. After Congress ratified the Treaty of Amity, Commerce, and Navigation, more commonly known as Jay's Treaty, in 1795, an agreement that settled border and trade issues with Great Britain, diplomatic tensions with America's former enemy seemed to ease. The French Republic, however, interpreted the treaty as favorable to Britain and thus as a hostile act by the United States. Consequently, France became more bellicose, and incidents at sea between American commercial vessels and French warships grew more common. Moreover, French agents fomented Indian hostilities on the southwestern frontier and began meddling in American domestic politics.

The growing antagonism with France, dubbed the Quasi-War, was aggravated by what came to be known as the XYZ Affair, in which French officials refused to receive American diplomats sent to Paris in 1797 by

◀ This map of the United States, dating from September 1796, shows the cluster of American towns and cities in the coastal Northwest. (Library of Congress)

51

The U.S. Army, 1783–1811

Washington's successor as president, John Adams, unless the ambassadors offered the officials bribes. Although he did not appeal to Congress for a declaration of war, Adams called for the provision of adequate resources for "the protection of our seafaring and commercial citizens; for the defense of any exposed portions of our territory; for replenishing our arsenals, establishing foundries, and military manufactures; and to provide ... efficient revenue" for military preparedness.

In June 1797, Congress responded to the war scare by appropriating additional funds for the construction of harbor forts. Since these installations would have to be garrisoned by soldiers, the legislature also turned its attention to the state of the Army. At the time, most of the troops remained scattered across the frontier, and in a poor state of readiness. Spread out in numerous small, isolated detachments, the Army was difficult to keep in proper order and discipline since it acted for the most part as a constabulary, rather than as a military force. Given the deplorable condition of the troops, Alexander Hamilton and other Federalists of a nationalist bent drafted a plan that called for the allocation of $1.1 million in funds and a force of twenty thousand regulars along with a provisional army of thirty thousand men. This was an

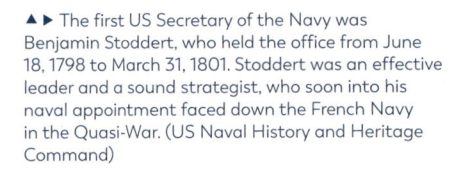

▲▶ The first US Secretary of the Navy was Benjamin Stoddert, who held the office from June 18, 1798 to March 31, 1801. Stoddert was an effective leader and a sound strategist, who soon into his naval appointment faced down the French Navy in the Quasi-War. (US Naval History and Heritage Command)

▶ A portrait of John Jay, one of the Founding Fathers of the United States, a signatory of the Treaty of Paris in 1783 and a senior statesman during the postwar years. (National Gallery of Art/PD)

Institutional Changes to Meet New Challenges, 1795–1800

◀ This British satirical artwork mocks Franco-American relations after the XYZ Affair in May of 1798. We see five Frenchmen violating and plundering the female figure of "America" while other national figures in the background do nothing. (Library of Congress)

▼ A fine portrait of Alexander Hamilton by John Trumbull in 1806. Hamilton served as the Army's inspector general and second in command and field commander in the late 1790s. (Google Arts and Culture/PD)

enormous number of soldiers, and if ratified, would dwarf the size of the nation's previous armies, which had rarely numbered over four thousand soldiers.

Congress did not adopt the Hamiltonian plan, but it did enact a number of provisions to put the nation on a war footing. Most of these laws exceeded what President Adams, himself a Federalist, thought necessary, and were opposed by mistrustful Republicans. In April 1798, an act passed for the raising of a new Regular Army regiment of artillery and engineers, to augment the Army's authorized strength of 3,870 men and 289 officers. The next month, Congress authorized $250,000 for additional fortification construction, $800,000 for arms and artillery procurement, and a three-year Provisional Army of ten thousand men, to be led by a lieutenant general and mobilized only in the event Congress declared war, if the country were invaded, or was in "imminent danger" of being attacked. In July, Congress increased the strength of the existing four regular infantry regiments, and added twelve new foot regiments and six troops of light dragoons, dubbed an Additional Army or New Army, to serve for the duration of the crisis with France. In a

The U.S. Army, 1783–1811

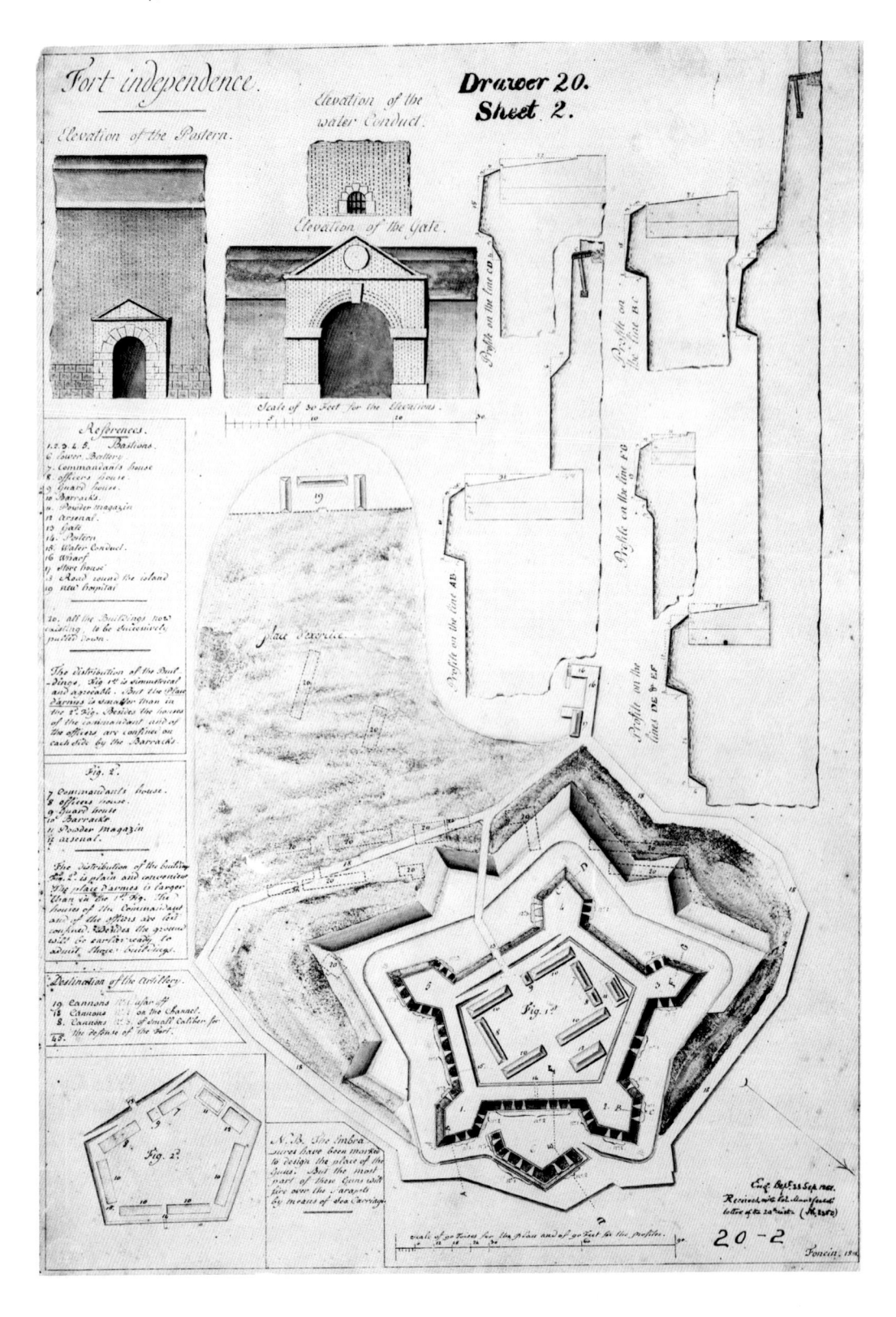

◀ Fort Independence on Castle Island, Boston, Massachusetts, took its name in 1799, although fortifications on the site dated back to the 17th century. This plan shows the fortress as it appeared in 1801. (Library of Congress)

break with tradition, this act created what was intended to be a strong federal force. The law dictated that officers' commissions come from the president, not from the states, and eliminated short-term enlistments, which had limited the Army's effectiveness since the early days of the Revolutionary War.

Largely due to the encouragement of Federalists who sought to frighten their political enemies, Congress authorized the president in March 1799 to raise thirty thousand more troops if war were declared or invasion seemed likely. Called the Eventual Army, this force was to be organized in twenty-four new infantry regiments, a regiment and a battalion of rifleman, three regiments of cavalry, and a battalion of engineers and artillerists. With enlistments not to exceed three years, the foot regiments were to consist of 1,026 men, 29 officers, and 10 cadets, while the artillery regiments would be slightly larger. The president could also accept into service a Provisional Army of seventy-five thousand men from the states, although once again, the officer commissions would come from federal authority, not from the states. These troops, however, could not be made to serve outside the states in which they enlisted, a provision that would have limited their use in the event of war and made them little different from militia.

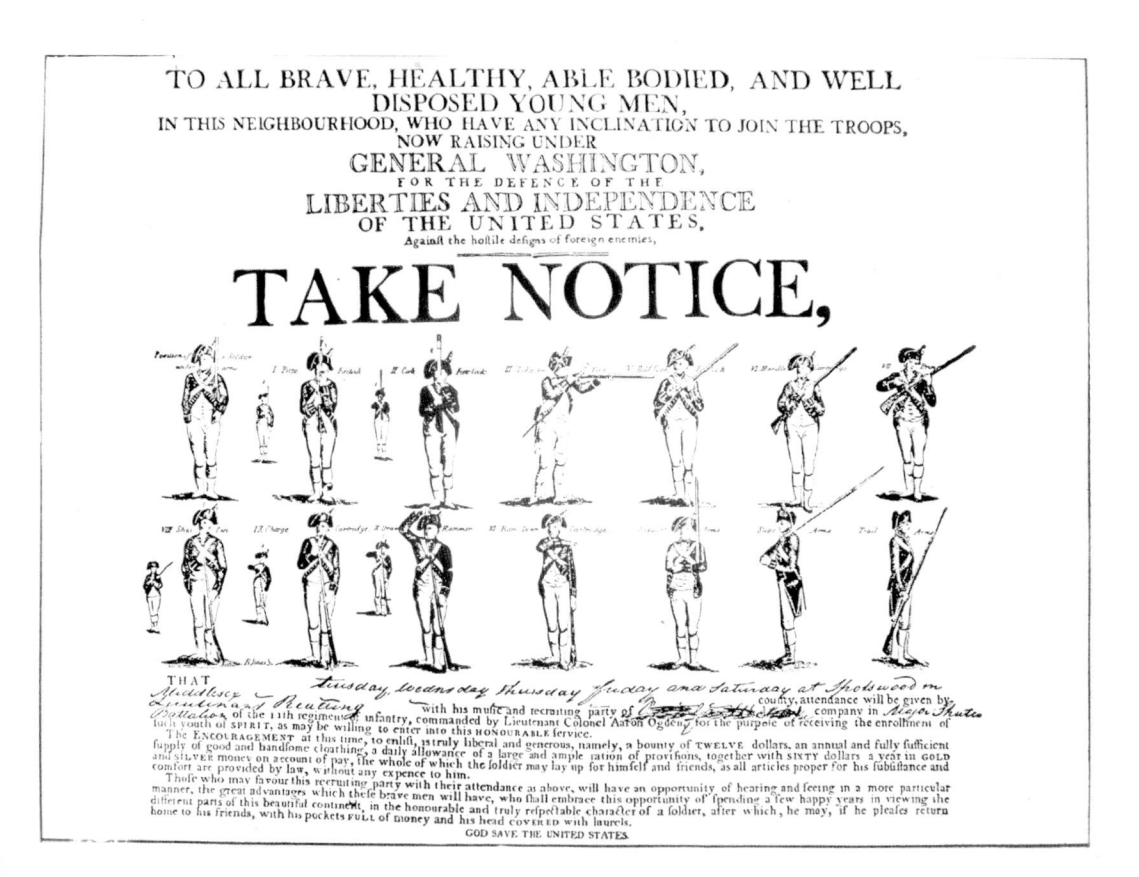

▼ As war with France seemed to threaten the United States in 1799, the U.S. government posted Army recruitment notices, this one utilizing Washington's revered name to encourage enlistment. (NARA)

Profile:
The Springfield Musket and Harpers Ferry Rifle

Between 1783 and 1811, a new musket entered service in the U.S. Army: the Springfield Model 1795. This was basically a U.S. copy of the Charleville Model 1763/66, with some marginal tweaks in design. It was the first musket to be produced by the great American inventor Eli Whitney at both the Springfield and Harpers Ferry armories; c. 15,000 were produced overall, and it became the mainstay musket of the War of 1812. The interwar period also saw the introduction of the first standard U.S. Army rifle, the Harpers Ferry Model 1803. In heavy .54 caliber, the M1803 had a 33 in or (later) 38 in barrel, much shorter than the Kentucky–Pennsylvania government-contract predecessors. This length reduction made the rifle less accurate over long ranges, but also more convenient to handle and less prone to barrel fouling. Pressure testing of these weapons in the War of 1812 led to new models and significant revisions, but the U.S. Army infantry entered the conflict adequately armed.

▼ A Springfield Model 1795–1808 musket. The quality of this musket is reflected in the fact that such weapons were still serving in the American Civil War, although by that time many had been converted to percussion cap ignition. (Smithsonian Institution)

◀▲ Model 1803 Harpers Ferry Rifle Officers Model. (Smithsonian Institution, National Museum of American History, Ralph G. Packard, CC0)

President Adams appointed George Washington to command the expanded Army, at the authorized rank of lieutenant general. Charles C. Pinckney and Alexander Hamilton received commissions as major generals, with Hamilton to serve as the Army's inspector general and second in command and field commander. In this role, Hamilton would oversee the mobilization and organization of the new Army instead of Washington, who remained at Mount Vernon, willing to serve only if the Army actually took the field. As it turned out, this new host never materialized. Despite the legislation of 1798 and 1799 to build a large Army, President Adams preferred to devote the country's military resources to strengthening the Navy, and paid little attention to the Army. Adams was wary of Hamilton's efforts to build up the Army when England posed little threat, and a French invasion was unlikely, given the ongoing European war. Adams suspected that Hamilton sought to use the Army for his own aggrandizement and to cow the Republican Party in its opposition to Federalist political objectives. Indeed, Hamilton made the regular force a politicized, Federalist institution by denying commissions to most Republicans.

Notwithstanding the war fever so prevalent within the ranks of his own party, Adams restarted negotiations with France in February 1799, hoping to preclude a full-scale conflict. The French were equally desirous to avert hostilities with the United States. As tensions eased, the effort to expand the Army quickly dissipated. Few enlistees joined the new regiments, and in February 1800, Congress suspended further enlistments. Three months later, President Adams ordered all the emergency soldiers to demobilize by June 15, with each discharged soldier to draw three months' pay and funds for his return home.

By the summer of 1800, the Regular Army was left with 3,429 men, serving on the western frontier and along the Atlantic seaboard in various posts and garrisons. On paper the force consisted of two regiments of artillerists and engineers, two troops of dragoons, and four infantry regiments, but the organizations rarely served together and were often below full strength. Congress repealed most of the military laws it had enacted over the prior two years. When Hamilton resigned his commission in June, General Wilkinson once again became the Army's senior officer, a position he was to hold until January 1812. In the fall of 1800, American diplomats signed a treaty with France, in which the latter recognized the neutrality of American ships and agreed to cease seizing commercial vessels engaged in legitimate trade. The Quasi-War was over.

The Army of the Early Jefferson Administration, 1801–1805

The turn of the century saw not only the end of the undeclared war with France, but also the election of Thomas Jefferson to the presidency. This period also marked a change in the dominant national political party, as Jefferson's Republicans took over power from the Federalists in both houses of Congress. The transition of chief executives inaugurated many changes in the country's political scene, including military affairs.

▼ Thomas Jefferson was president of the United States between 1801 and 1809. He was the driving force behind the Military Peace Establishment Act of March 16, 1802. (White House Historical Association/PD)

Reorganizing the Army

Jefferson's views on the proper role of a standing army in the American political system have often been mischaracterized by historians. He was philosophically opposed to a standing army in peacetime on the grounds that it was expensive to maintain and was dangerous to individual liberties. Jefferson did, however, recognize that some military force was necessary to protect the young republic from external threats. He also saw the need to train engineers and artillerists, to avoid a reliance on foreign-born and foreign-educated officers. Jefferson did not seek to dismantle the Regular Army, but expected to use state militias as a first line of defense. He regarded America's armed forces as "defensive,"

The Army of the Early Jefferson Administration, 1801–1805

and sought to avoid entanglements in foreign disputes, particularly with France, England, and Spain, all of which he regarded as prospective threats to American security. Thus, Jefferson's opposition to a large standing army in time of peace was based on pragmatic utility about expenses as much as it was on ideological fervor.

Henry Dearborn, secretary of war during both of Jefferson's presidential terms, shared the president's views on the military establishment and was instrumental in bringing about the changes Jefferson desired. A Revolutionary War veteran and former congressman, Dearborn favored a small, well-trained force of regulars to defend against enemy invasion and for frontier duty, with the militia maintaining internal order as needed. Jefferson relied on Dearborn for advice on military matters nearly to the exclusion of all others, including the Army's senior officer, General Wilkinson.

▲ Henry Dearborn, by Walter M. Brackett. (U.S. Army Art Collection)

By the time Jefferson assumed office, war between England and France had cooled, while America's diplomatic relations with these two nations had improved. Without a direct threat looming, Congress could reduce America's military establishment in the interest of economy. The president and his fellow Republicans also hoped to remodel the Army to ensure its loyalty, make certain it would not be a threat to the new regime, and embrace Republican principles. At the time Jefferson took office, the Army's officer corps was a Federalist stronghold. Jefferson feared that the politicized Army would form a determined opposition to his policies, and indeed most of the officers were hostile to the new administration.

Beginning in 1802, Republicans used the annual appropriations process to tailor the armed forces to more limited defensive roles, reducing military spending by about one-third. Congress' reorganization of the Army in 1802 called for significant cuts in the authorized strength of the armed forces. Congress also cut Army staff positions to eliminate some of the more partisan Federalist senior officers.

The president likewise consolidated Army units to reduce the need for field officers. Finally, Jefferson created the rank of colonel for the infantry regiments

The U.S. Army, 1783–1811

and the Corps of Artillery, which allowed him to appoint men of his own political sentiments to these positions.

Since the Army never reached the authorized strength of 5,438 men, the 1802 bill did little to actually reduce the size of the Army. On December 19, 1801, the Army had 248 officers, 9 cadets, and 3,794 enlisted men in four regiments of infantry, two of artillery and engineers, and two companies of light dragoons. Thus, when the new legislation placed a troop limit of 3,289 (a 40-percent decrease), it meant an actual reduction of only several hundred men. With the assistance of his personal secretary, Lt. Meriwether Lewis, President Jefferson evaluated all officers for their political reliability. Ultimately he dismissed about one-third of the Army's officers after the Military Peace Establishment Act of 1802, and most of them—seventy-six officers—were Federalists. By June 1 of that year, the Army had 172 officers, and an authorized enlisted strength of 3,040 men, although fewer were actually present for duty.

Meanwhile, Congress established a new entity, the U.S. Army Corps of Engineers, through the Military Peace Establishment Act of 1802. The organization consisted of ten cadets and seven officers, and was located at West Point. Lawmakers intended for the Corps to form a military academy, the superintendent of which was to be the Army's chief engineer. Jefferson and the Republicans had initially opposed the plan to create a military college, but after 1800, they embraced the idea as a reform measure. This effort attempted to end American reliance on foreign engineers for technical military expertise. Additionally, the establishment

▼ Long Barracks at West Point, by unknown artist. (West Point Museum Collections, United States Military Academy)

West Point as it appeared in 1904, just over 100 years after its original founding in March 1802. (Internet Archive Book Images)

of the academy at West Point advanced Jefferson's "republicanization" of the Army, as the new school would train young men loyal to Republican principles for service in the Army. Under the Jefferson administration, most cadet appointments went to Republican families. The act further allowed the president to select the officers who would teach at West Point, thereby further solidifying his control over the school's ideological bent.

Helping to Build the Nation

Jefferson's support for a Corps of Engineers also reflected his philosophy that the Army should perform services beneficial to the new nation. He believed that in peacetime the Army's mission went beyond defense to include "building the nation." Such opportunities were not long in coming. Army troops built military roads between Lake Erie and Lake Ontario, and within the Creek Indian lands of Mississippi and Alabama. Soldiers not only improved and expanded the Natchez Trace, linking Nashville with the Mississippi River, but they also provided small garrisons along the trail to protect travelers from outlaws.

Jefferson called upon the Army again when he purchased the Louisiana Territory from France in 1803. The purchase included over 825,000 square miles of land, including portions of what would become fifteen U.S. states and two Canadian provinces, most of which had never been explored by Europeans or Americans. To rectify this situation, Jefferson authorized what became known as the Lewis and Clark

Expedition. The president decided to use the Army for this mission, both because the military had experience in sustaining lengthy and difficult expeditions, and because the military could represent the power and authority of the federal government in a manner a civilian exploratory effort would not. The president chose recently promoted Capt. Meriwether Lewis, his personal secretary and Virginia neighbor, to lead the effort. Lewis selected William Clark to serve as his co-leader, although he actually ranked as a lieutenant. Clark was a former Army infantry officer who had fought in Anthony Wayne's campaign in Ohio before resigning his commission in 1796.

Jefferson's purpose was to find an all-water northwest passage across the continent to the Pacific, to establish friendly relations with western Indians, to help expand American trade, and to gather natural information on the west's plants, animals, and geography. Finally, the president had a national security motive. In the South, Spain, fearful that the United States would invade northern Mexico and capture its silver mines, sought to prevent Americans from moving westward from the lower Mississippi River. To the north, Jefferson was concerned that Canadian fur trappers working in the Rockies and northern plains would prompt Great Britain to lay formal claim to the area. Finally, he wished to learn what threat the Indian tribes west of the Mississippi might pose to future American expansion.

The expedition lasted two years and four months, and covered 7,689 miles. Thirty-four soldiers initially accompanied Lewis and Clark on the journey, twenty-six of whom traveled all the way to the Pacific coast. Beginning at St. Louis, the group started up the Missouri River in May 1804. There were several tense encounters on the Great Plains upon encountering the Teton Sioux, but the party managed to pass, and wintered the first year at the Mandan villages on the upper Missouri River in what is now North Dakota. The explorers kept detailed journals, produced excellent maps of their journey, and collected specimens of

▲ ▶ Portraits of Meriwether Lewis (above) and William Clark (right), by Charles Willson Peale. (Independence National Historical Park, Philadelphia)

Profile:
U.S. Army Corps of Engineers

The importance of military engineers became evident to both sides during the War of Independence. On the rebel side, Colonel Richard Gridley was appointed as the chief engineer to the New England Provincial Army, and in July 1775 he rose to become chief angineer (artillery) within the newly created Continental Army. In 1779, Congress went further and established a specific Corps of Engineers, which played a critical role in the remainder of the war.

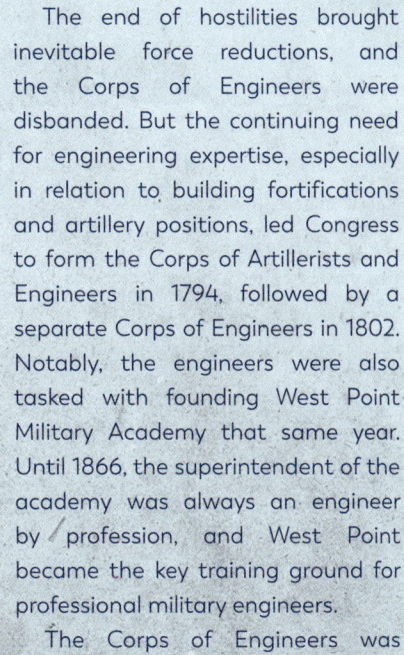

The end of hostilities brought inevitable force reductions, and the Corps of Engineers were disbanded. But the continuing need for engineering expertise, especially in relation to building fortifications and artillery positions, led Congress to form the Corps of Artillerists and Engineers in 1794, followed by a separate Corps of Engineers in 1802. Notably, the engineers were also tasked with founding West Point Military Academy that same year. Until 1866, the superintendent of the academy was always an engineer by profession, and West Point became the key training ground for professional military engineers.

The Corps of Engineers was put to work on both military and government-direct civil projects. Thus as well as building fortifications, barracks and military hospitals they also constructed bridges, lighthouses and harbor facilities. Between 1807 and 1812, defensive construction dominated their efforts as the possibility of another continental war loomed. The chief engineer during this time was Colonel Jonathan Williams, who held the post concurrently with that of superintendent of West Point.

◀ An artwork by H. Charles McBarron, Jr., shows construction work near West Point in 1805. The soldier in the foreground is an artillery cadet, wearing the mixture of commissioned and non-commissioned uniforms prescribed for cadets of artillery. (U.S. Center of Military History)

dozens of plants and animals. The soldiers traversed the vast open plains and the rugged Rocky Mountains the next year, and spent the second winter by the Pacific Ocean at the mouth of the Columbia River, where they established Fort Clatsop. They left the West Coast in March 1806 to return home and reached St. Louis on September 23, 1806. Spanish authorities, secretly informed of the Corps of Discovery's mission by none other than the U.S. Army's senior officer, General Wilkinson—a paid Spanish informant—attempted to capture Lewis and Clark as they traveled up the Missouri River, but failed to intercept them.

Lewis and Clark's western expedition was the most extensive exploration of the western territory, but it was not the only such operation at the time. Capt. Zebulon M. Pike led a foray in 1805 north from St. Louis to the upper reaches of the Mississippi River to map waterways, to examine wildlife and vegetation, and to send back "whatever curiosities" the men collected. There was an unwritten military reconnaissance aspect of this mission as well, in which Pike, a veteran of the battle at Fallen Timbers, was to clear out British fur traders in the region, apparently with the encouragement of Secretary Dearborn and General Wilkinson. The following year, Pike and Lt. James B. Wilkinson, the general's son, set out together to scout routes to northern Mexico, to gather intelligence, and to discover the courses of several major rivers, including the Red, which would put the soldiers close to the Spanish stronghold of Santa Fe. On the Arkansas River, Pike turned west searching for the Rocky Mountains with twenty men, and sent Lieutenant Wilkinson with a handful of soldiers to report back to his father. Pike reached the Rockies in what is now Colorado by November, but by then harsh weather made for severe hardships for his party. In February 1807, a detachment of Spanish soldiers found the Americans, escorted them to Santa Fe, on to Mexico, and eventually back to U.S. soil.

◀ In this artwork dating to 1810, "Captains Lewis & Clark hold a council with the Indians." One of the primary missions of the expedition was to observe and record information about Native American culture. (Library of Congress)

While exploratory missions in the West occupied a small part of the Army and a large part of Jefferson's intellectual interests, most of America's land forces were located at key posts in Louisiana. The U.S. Army took formal possession of Louisiana on December 20, 1803, establishing garrisons at New Orleans and several smaller posts on the southern waters of the Mississippi River. The Army sent over four hundred men in six artillery companies and four infantry companies of the 2d Infantry to occupy New Orleans, an isolated but strategic post. Due to the uncertain loyalties of the French populace in New Orleans, U.S. Army regulars were essential to its defense. The new territory consisted of two administrative districts, Orleans in the south and Louisiana to the north. Capt. Amos Stoddard served as the district commandant at St. Louis, headquarters of the Louisiana District, to "exercise civil as well as military powers until a territorial government could be organized." General Wilkinson received the appointment of governor of the Louisiana Territory. At the same time, William C. C. Claiborne, formerly governor of the Mississippi Territory, became Orleans Territory governor.

Securing the Spanish Frontier

Although the Louisiana Purchase removed France as a potential threat to the new nation, another, Spain, remained. The primary threat to American interests early in Jefferson's administration was Spanish presence in the Floridas and in lands west of the Mississippi River, unsettlingly close to New Orleans. As recently as October 1802, the Spanish had closed the port of New Orleans to American goods coming down the Mississippi, and they had also denied the U.S. government's request to supply Fort Stoddert in the Mississippi Territory by passing through Louisiana free of duties. Consequently, upon ratification of the Louisiana Purchase, President Jefferson moved troops to southern Louisiana to deter any potential Spanish advance in the region. (See Map 2.)

Spanish possession of East and West Florida likewise posed a danger to American security and prosperity in the South. Settlers in the Mississippi Territory, which also included the future state of Alabama, needed access to the port town of Mobile in Spanish territory in order to send their agricultural products to market. As with New Orleans, the Spanish could cripple American affluence in the region by limiting access to harbors on the Gulf Coast. Jefferson alternatively tried to bully and bribe Spain to part with the Floridas, and even concentrated troops along the Mississippi border with West Florida at Fort Stoddert. Despite the bluff, Jefferson failed to secure this territory for the United States.

Over the next several months, American soldiers occupied additional military posts, including Concordia, across the Mississippi River from Natchez; Plaquemines, upstream from New Orleans; and Balize, on the Gulf of Mexico. A small contingent of soldiers in March 1804 also occupied the Arkansas Post at

The U.S. Army, 1783–1811

The Army of the Early Jefferson Administration, 1801–1805

the mouth of the Arkansas River, and Fort Miro on the Washita River, the following month. American forces took over Natchitoches, an old French settlement on the Red River, from a small Spanish garrison in April, and renamed it Fort Claiborne, garrisoning it with one hundred seventy regulars by the end of the year. By late 1804, almost seven hundred soldiers occupied nine outposts or forts in the Louisiana Territory.

Unfortunately, the border between American Louisiana and Spanish possessions in Mexico had not been firmly established. Jefferson held that the border was the Sabine River, and Wilkinson recommended the establishment of Army posts on this river to counter the Spanish, who regarded the boundary as being eighty miles farther east. In this uncertainty, Dearborn directed Wilkinson to prepare plans for an invasion of Spanish territory, should such a contingency become necessary. In October 1805, one thousand Spanish troops marched eastward and occupied two forts east of the Sabine River near Natchitoches. The United States regarded the move as a hostile territorial encroachment. Jefferson responded by ordering soldiers along the frontier "to be in readiness to protect our citizens, and to repel by arms" any Spanish aggression.

◀ Artist Charles Marion Russell shows the moment Lewis and Clark meet Native Americans on the Lower Columbia River. (Humanities Texas/PD)

LOWER MISSISSIPPI THEATER
1803–1811

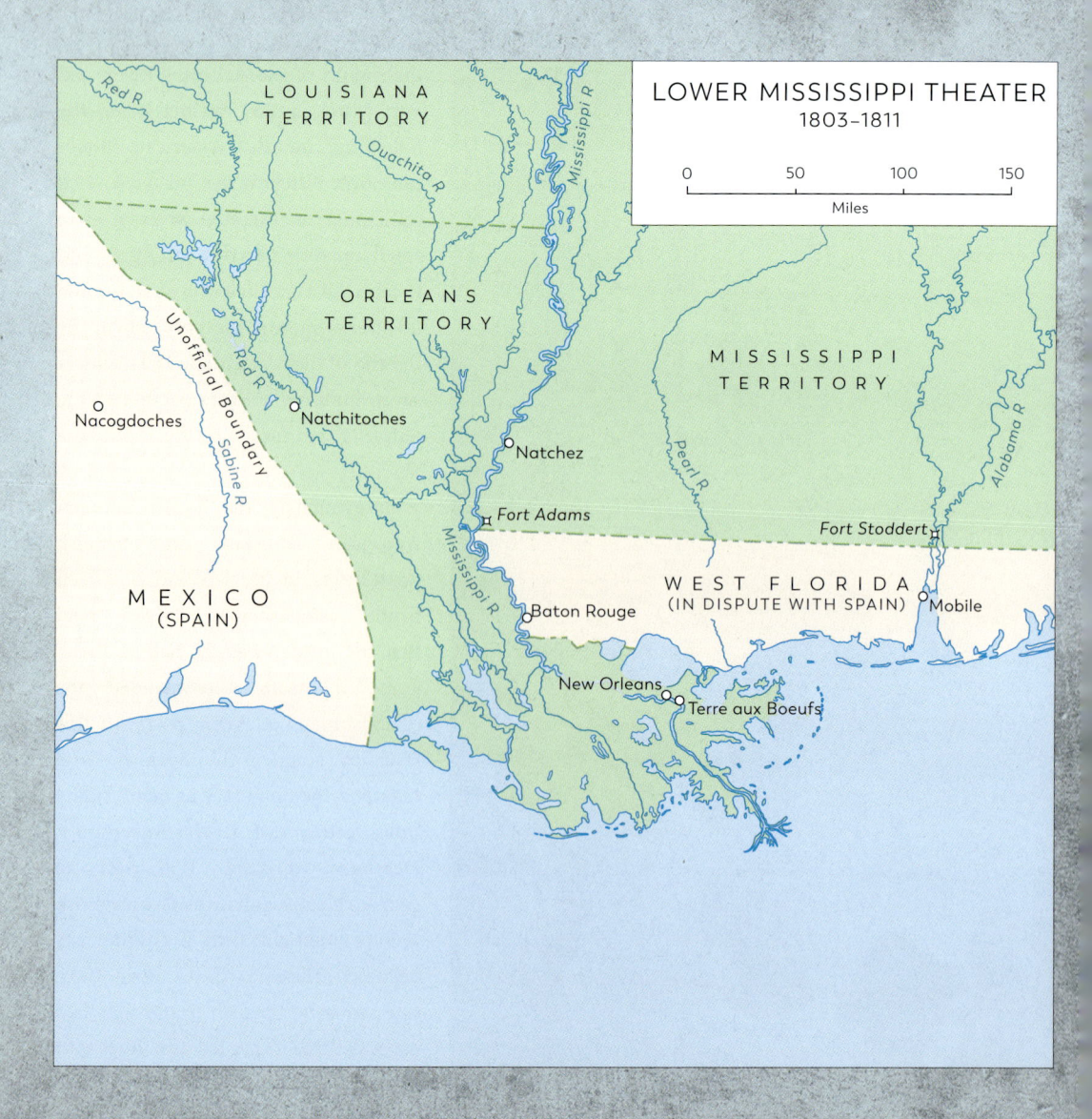

▲ Map 2

The Army of the Early Jefferson Administration, 1801–1805

In January 1806, Lt. William Piatt led a small force of American soldiers to the Spanish garrison of Nacogdoches, Mexico, to demand that the Spanish recognize the Sabine River as the international border and to withdraw all of their forces to the west of it. The garrison commander refused to comply. The following month, an Army detachment under Capt. Edward D. Turner advanced against Bayou Pierre, a Spanish post northwest of Natchitoches, and forced the Spanish troops there to withdraw west of the Sabine. In March, Wilkinson ordered Col. Thomas Cushing of the 2d Infantry to move up the Red River to Natchitoches with three companies and two field pieces to bolster American forces there, although Cushing was ordered not to provoke a conflict. In the spring, Wilkinson received orders

▼ Displayed in the American Heritage Museum, this 1795 6-pounder cannon is representative of the horse-drawn light field artillery that accompanied U.S. troops on many of their campaigns. (Joshbaumgartner/CC BY-SA 4.0)

from Washington to move from his St. Louis headquarters to New Orleans, to take charge of the tense situation personally, but the general delayed leaving St. Louis until late August. Wilkinson joined Cushing on September 22 at Natchitoches with enough additional troops to bring the force there to twelve hundred men, and sent a message to the nearby Spanish commander, Col. Simon de Herrera, to abandon his nearby position. Fighting seemed imminent, although Wilkinson had too few troops to launch an extended campaign across the Sabine against Herrera's one thousand men. By early fall, the Spanish defused the situation by withdrawing to Nacogdoches, and in November leaders of both belligerents had established a neutral buffer zone fifty miles wide between the Sabine River and the Arroyo Hondo to the east, which Spain claimed was the actual border. With hostilities now unlikely, Wilkinson returned to New Orleans by November 22, while Maj. Moses Porter of the artillery marched most of the soldiers there as well, leaving one company of troops to garrison Natchitoches. No further military flare-ups occurred in the region, but the Jefferson administration and Congress kept a watchful eye on the Spanish positions at Baton Rouge, Mobile, Pensacola, and along the Sabine River.

The Army and the Second Jefferson Administration, 1805–1809

No sooner had tensions with Spain begun to ease than new dangers surfaced to threaten the young nation. The first took the form of an internal conspiracy to slice off a significant portion of the United States to form a new state or even nation. The second, more traditional in form, was renewed confrontation with Great Britain over British actions on the high seas.

▼ Aaron Burr, by John Vanderlyn, 1802. (New York Historical Society)

The Burr Conspiracy

In 1805, Jefferson's former vice president, Aaron Burr, began formulating a scheme to carve a new empire out of American and Spanish territory in the West. Although his plans remain murky to this day, he hoped to seize New Orleans with a force of volunteers recruited along the Ohio River frontier. Once in control of the city, he planned to separate Louisiana and other western states and territories from the United States, move into West Florida and northeastern Mexico, and add those mostly unsettled Spanish possessions to a new realm. Presumably, Burr would lead the new independent empire, as a way of reviving his political fortunes after having mortally wounded Alexander Hamilton in an 1804 duel. Burr succeeded in enticing several officers of Western garrisons into his scheme. By far his most powerful co-conspirator, however, was none other than the commanding general of the U.S. Army and governor of the Louisiana Territory, General Wilkinson.

The former vice president expected the general to use his soldiers to participate in his secession schemes by securing New Orleans and invading Spanish-held territory. The conflict with Spain in the southwest provided Wilkinson cover to redeploy troops to critical areas in Louisiana to bolster Burr and Wilkinson's plans of removing the Spanish threat and establishing a separate western empire along the lower Mississippi and in Texas. Burr began to put his plan into effect in the summer of 1806, but quickly lost support from his backers, many of whom now regarded his design as foolhardy. After he received a warning from Dearborn to steer clear of Burr, Wilkinson double-crossed him in the fall of 1806, advising President Jefferson of all he knew of the conspiracy, while concealing his own role in Burr's machinations. Prior to Burr's capture, Wilkinson moved most of his troops along the southern Mississippi to New Orleans and bolstered the city's defenses with militia units to prevent the conspirators from taking it by force.

President Jefferson regarded Burr's plan as both a filibustering expedition against northern Mexico and a treasonous attack against American possessions in the new Louisiana Territory. Once convinced of the serious nature of Burr's plot, the president

▲ A military service record for one John Edlin, Parke's Squadron, Light Dragoons, Militia, operating in Indian Territory in 1811. (National Archives/PD)

commanded all civil and military officers to help quash the former vice president's activities under the 1794 Neutrality Act, which made it illegal for an American citizen to wage war against any country at peace with the United States. The War Department also sent orders to Army garrisons along the Ohio and Mississippi rivers to arrest Burr and his conspirators, and otherwise suppress the illegal venture. A small detachment of soldiers from Fort Stoddert led by Lt. Francis P. Gaines eventually apprehended Burr in the Mississippi Territory in February 1807. Much to Jefferson's chagrin, a jury acquitted him of all charges in September 1807.

For a time the situation along the Mississippi was "urgent and critical," but with Burr in custody, his scheme collapsed. Wilkinson tried to portray himself as the savior of the western lands. Despite being suspected of duplicitous conduct with Burr and Spanish authorities, in June 1808 a military board of inquiry exonerated him after six months of hearings. Jefferson nevertheless removed Wilkinson from his position as governor of the Louisiana Territory, replacing him with Meriwether Lewis. Jefferson and Dearborn also faced the unwelcome fact that many Army officers serving in the west had sympathized with Burr's conspiracy, and some of them had openly supported it. In the end, in part due to the threats posed to the United States by both Spain and France, Jefferson decided not to purge the officer corps of those whom he suspected of being part of Burr's cause.

The *Chesapeake* Affair and the Expansion of the Army, 1807–1809

While the prosecution of Aaron Burr proceeded during the summer of 1807, an incident involving the Navy in waters off the Virginia coast suddenly shifted the attention of the Jefferson administration from the Spanish in the southwest to the British in the Atlantic. The event not only affected the strength and organization of the Army, but it also was a contributing factor to the outbreak of war five years later between the United States and Great Britain. On June 22, 1807, the U.S. Navy frigate *Chesapeake* sailed from Hampton Roads, Virginia, bound for the Mediterranean Sea. Several hours later, the *Chesapeake* encountered the British frigate *Leopard*, which stopped the American vessel and demanded that Royal Navy officers be allowed to board and search for deserters. When *Chesapeake*'s captain refused, *Leopard* fired three broadsides at the ship, killing three and wounding eighteen of the crew. Unprepared for battle, *Chesapeake* surrendered without firing a shot, and allowed the British to search the ship, during which time Royal Navy officers discovered and removed four alleged British deserters, although only one was actually a British subject. Once the ship returned to Hampton Roads, news of the humiliating event spread quickly, and Americans were outraged at the attack on their vessel in American waters and the violation of the nation's sovereignty. Jefferson, Dearborn, and Wilkinson began to work on defensive plans, although the president wanted to "avoid ... every act which would precipitate general hostilities."

As war fever grew across America, Dearborn recommended augmenting the Army to fifteen thousand troops, in addition to thirty-two thousand volunteers to serve for three months, primarily for training under the War Department's authority. Jefferson was slower to act. He understood the pitfalls of depending on militia organizations to defend the country, especially since his numerous calls for reforms of the militia system had gone unheeded during his presidency. He called a special session of Congress to react to the *Chesapeake* affair, but made no recommendations to Congress, which took up the issues of harbor defenses, naval preparations, and the militia. A few members of Congress maintained the traditional Republican opposition to a strong standing force, while others joined in with harsh criticism of the Army's role in supporting Burr's plot "to dismember the Union." In February 1808, Jefferson advised Congress of his plan to enlarge the nation's military establishment. This included raising an additional 6,000 soldiers to bring the authorized strength of the Army to just over 9,000 men. The president also recommended creation of an additional force of 24,000 volunteers to serve twelve months, armed and equipped by the federal government. After some objections from traditionalists over the size of the force, particularly since the United States was not then at war with any nation, Congress approved $4 million to augment the Army and militia and to construct 188 gunboats to defend the country's seaports. The Army's strength reached 2,775 men in 1807, and 5,712 the next year, although recruiting was slow. The increase in regiments not only meant more men in the ranks, but also more opportunities for the Jefferson administration to appoint Republican officers to lead them, men of firm Republican sympathies, who would pose no problems as did those officers on the western frontier who had supported Aaron Burr. Few men of a Federalist bent received appointments,

◀ The USS *Chesapeake* (right) and HMS *Leopard* exchange shots off the Virginia coast on June 22, 1807, after the British captain refused to allow the Americans on board to search for deserters. (The Mariners' Museum, Newport News, Virginia)

and by the end of the year, Republicans made up a majority of the officer corps. The Army reached a strength of about 5,700 troops, although many recruits were "miserable wretches" lacking "discipline and order."

Meanwhile, Jefferson struck a nonviolent blow at nations that refused to recognize American maritime rights. In late 1807 and early 1808, Congress passed three embargo acts. These acts banned American ships from engaging in most foreign trade in an attempt to coerce Britain and France to stop their mutual harassment of American neutral shipping and, in the case of Britain, the impressment of seamen on American vessels. The effort backfired in that it caused severe economic hardship in the United States, particularly in the Northeast where Federalists were numerous.

Due to the widespread practice of smuggling on land and sea to avoid the provisions of the embargo, Jefferson called on the Army and Navy to enforce Congress' commercial restrictions. Although Jefferson had strongly opposed the use of a federal Army to suppress the Whiskey Rebellion in 1794, he signed a law in March 1807 authorizing the use of regulars to put down domestic disorders, including "all

▶ The USS *Chesapeake* was a 38-gun frigate laid down in December 1798 and launched almost exactly one year later. The ship's American career ended in June 1813, when it was captured by the British. (Courtesy of the U.S. Navy Art Collection, Washington, D.C. U.S. Naval History and Heritage Command Photograph)

The Army and the Second Jefferson Administration, 1805–1809

cases of insurrection or obstruction to the laws." In the summer of 1808, the president ordered General Wilkinson to send recruits to the Canadian border to assist U.S. customs officers enforcing the trade ban and to battle "the armed resistance to the embargo laws" from Maine to Detroit. Three companies of untried regulars in New York marched from their training camps to Sackets Harbor, Oswegatchie, and Plattsburgh to enforce the embargo in place of the state militia, whose members often sympathized with the smugglers. Treasury Secretary Albert Gallatin observed in July that "we must depend entirely on force for checking this manner of violating the law," and to prevent smuggling along the Great Lakes, "nothing but force on land ... will put a stop to the violations." He recommended to Jefferson that "we must have a little army along the Lakes and British lines generally," since along the border "the people are now there altogether against the law."

▲ Albert Gallatin was the U.S. treasury secretary between 1801 and 1814. (Metropolitan Museum of Art)

By early 1809, opposition to the embargo became so strong that Congress passed the "Force Bill," which authorized Jefferson to use the federal military establishment and state militias to enforce American commercial laws. The act generated opposition in much of the country, particularly among those who resented federal interference with the state militia organizations. Jefferson declared entire towns to be in a state of treason for opposition to his embargo in the form of civil disobedience. In the face of public opposition to the acts, Congress repealed them in the closing days of the Jefferson administration. In their place, the legislature enacted the Non-Intercourse Law of 1809 that banned trade just with France and Britain. Enforcement of this law was no easier than its predecessors, and smuggling remained rampant. Ultimately, Jefferson's experiment with coercive trade policies, in which the U.S. Army found itself in the role of enforcer against the people, failed miserably.

Clouds on the Horizon, 1809–1812

James Madison of Virginia was inaugurated on March 4, 1809 as the fourth president of the United States. William Eustis, an Army surgeon during the Revolutionary War, became Madison's new secretary of war. Together they faced an increasingly tense situation both with Native Americans on the northwestern frontier and with Great Britain, which continued to refuse to recognize the rights of American neutral shipping. These developments led American leaders to consider how the United States should best prepare for war.

In early 1810, Secretary Eustis favored enlisting fifty thousand volunteers, who would be equipped and armed by the federal government, and led by officers appointed by the president. Six thousand of these men were to be in artillery and rifle companies. At the same time, President Madison asked Congress to mobilize up to one hundred thousand militiamen to fill out Regular Army regiments up to their authorized limits. He also requested an additional force of twenty thousand short-term volunteers to be available on short notice. The projected cost for these measures was $6,037,000, a huge sum given the decreased federal revenues as a result of the various economic measures enacted by Congress over the past several years. Congress rejected these requests. Instead, it granted the president the power to call on the states for militia if necessary, but otherwise, it did little to strengthen the regular force.

In the summer of 1811, Madison and the Republicans in Congress pressed for war preparations and finances. In late November, 1811, the Army consisted of 5,447 men located at twenty-three posts, still commanded by General James Wilkinson, with most of the soldiers stationed near New Orleans. Madison hoped to fill up the ranks of the regulars to the authorized strength of 10,603 soldiers, create an auxiliary force of regulars, increase arms manufacturing within the United States,

Profile:
William Eustis (1753–1825)

William Eustis was born on June 10, 1753, in Cambridge, Massachusetts. He was academically minded, graduating from Harvard in 1772 then studying medicine under Dr Joseph Warren, later a pivotal leader in the American Revolution. Eustis settled into medical practice in Boston, but with the outbreak of war in 1775 he served on the front lines as a field surgeon for revolutionary militia and the troops of the Continental Army. He also established a military hospital near New York City. After the war, Eustis returned to his Boston practice, although he also supported American militia troops fighting in Shays' Rebellion in 1787. But his post-war career was defined mainly by political rather than military office. From 1788 to 1794 he was a member of the Massachusetts House of Representatives, then of the U.S. House of Representatives from 1801 to 1805 and 1820 to 1823, as a Democratic-Republican. Between his spells in U.S. Congress, he served for four years (1809–1813) as the secretary of war under President James Madison, one of the least successful parts of his career, and from 1814 to 1819 was the minister to the Netherlands. The final act of his political career began when he was elected governor of Massachusetts in 1823, after three previous failed attempts. He died in office, of pneumonia, on February 6, 1825.

◀ William Eustis, by Walter M. Brackett (U.S. Army Art Collection)

and obtain supplies for state militias. After debating a number of proposals from the House of Representatives and President Madison, in January 1812, Congress voted to raise 25,000 new men for the Regular Army in thirteen regiments of 2,000 men each. It also approved the creation of a volunteer force of 30,000 men, financed by a $1 million appropriation, although the War Department had previously called for 50,000 volunteers. In April 1812, Congress also called on the state governors to have 80,000 militiamen ready for defensive service within the United States. Two months later, on the eve of declaring war with Great Britain, Congress authorized two new brigadier generals and reduced the regular regiments to 1,000 men each.

During the months after Congress enacted legislation to raise volunteers, recruiting remained slow, which led to the need for more regulars. By the summer of 1812, the regulars numbered only 6,744. Madison found it far easier to raise generals than enlisted men. He appointed former Secretary of War Henry Dearborn as senior major general, while Thomas Pinckney of South Carolina also received a major generalship, with headquarters in Charleston. The administration appointed several new brigadier generals, including William Hull, Joseph Bloomfield, James Winchester, Thomas Flournoy, and John Chandler. Lower-ranking officers of quality and experience, as well as the proper political allegiance to please Madison and the Republicans, were hard to find, and most Revolutionary War veterans were no longer fit for active service. The Madison administration accepted some Federalists in cases when it was unable to find politically palatable men, although such attempts at bipartisanship irked hard-line Jeffersonians.

The Northwestern Frontier and the Battle of Tippecanoe

While Congress moved tentatively to prepare for a possible war with Great Britain, the persistent demand for more land by American settlers continued to alienate the Indians of the Northwest.

▼ Tenskwatawa is portrayed in *Ten-squat-a-way, the Open Door, Known as the Prophet, Brother of Tecumseh*, by George Catlin, 1830. (Smithsonian American Art Museum)

As William Henry Harrison, the governor and commander in chief of the Indiana Territory, superintendent of Indian affairs, and commissioner plenipotentiary of the United States, wrote: "I wish I could say the Indians were treated with justice and propriety on all occasions by our citizens, but it is far otherwise. They are often abused and mistreated." The growing friction between land-hungry whites and the indigenous people led to a resurgent pan-Indian movement to defend native lands and ways of life. Two prominent leaders of the movement included Tenskwatawa, a religious prophet, and his brother Tecumseh, considered to be the movement's military chief. In 1805, Tenskwatawa gathered a new community of adherents at Prophetstown, at the confluence of the Wabash and Tippecanoe Rivers, in the Indiana Territory. The gathering at Prophetstown of a large number of Indians alarmed Harrison and other American leaders, who began to consider steps to eradicate the native threat.

Enmity against encroaching whites increased after some Indian leaders agreed to a treaty at Fort Wayne in September 1809, in which American negotiators led by Harrison obtained from the Miami, Potawatomi, Lenape, and Eel

The U.S. Army, 1783–1811

River Indians approximately three million acres mainly in Indiana's Wabash Valley, north of Vincennes. Tecumseh and Tenskwatawa objected that the Indian signatories did not have the authority to sign the treaty, and could not rightfully sell land commonly held with other native peoples. By 1810, Indian raids against white farms and settlements increased, as the Prophetstown leaders continued to spread the message of resistance to white intrusions into native lands. Tecumseh and Tenskwatawa captured the annual salt provisions provided by the United States to several friendly Indian tribes and sought to procure arms from the British.

Rumors circulated on the frontier that the Indians planned to wipe out all settlers. President Madison feared that a western Indian war would make a potential war

◄ Tecumseh, a Shawnee Native American leader, vigorously resisted the American settler expansion, leading a massive Indian confederacy from c. 1808. (Toronto Public Library/PD)

with Great Britain more difficult, and thus urged Harrison to avoid hostilities with natives. Harrison met with Tecumseh in order to resolve issues over land and the tide of settlers coming into western Indiana, but the talks accomplished little. By 1811, Harrison began to prepare for war with the Indians of Prophetstown. He placed little faith in the militia organization of the Indiana Territory. Instead, the territorial governor requested federal troops to defend the territory, and if need be, to join an offensive against the Indians. Reluctantly, Madison and Eustis agreed to send the newly raised 4th Infantry under Lt. Col. John Parker Boyd to Vincennes to protect settlers. Many of the regiment's new men were "seamen who had been thrown out of work by the embargo." One observer claimed the regiment was "composed of the best materiel I had ever seen in any service." Nevertheless, these men were "raw troops." When Harrison learned that Tecumseh planned to travel to various southern Indian tribes that fall, he recognized an opportunity to eradicate Prophetstown while the Indian military chief was gone. Along with the 4th Infantry, by October Harrison had mustered twelve hundred men, including one detached company of the 7th Infantry, a company of the Rifle Regiment (armed at the time with muskets), Indiana militia, mounted riflemen, and one hundred twenty dragoons from Kentucky and Indiana. Although Tenskwatawa made no overtly threatening moves against Harrison's command at Vincennes, the governor ordered his forces northward on September 27 "through an uninhabited country" toward Prophetstown, the army "being well furnished with arms, ammunition and provision." The army's march was "slow and cautious" as great care was taken to avoid ambushes, while most of the heavy baggage went by water. The soldiers marched in "two columns or files on either side of the road, and the mounted riflemen and cavalry in front, in the rear, and on the flanks," reported Lt. Charles Larrabee. Three days later, the column reached the Wabash River at Battelle des Illinois, where the men camped and constructed a stockade they named Fort Harrison and several nearby blockhouses. Harrison went so far as to stage a mock battle near this camp, to give his green soldiers some idea of what to expect once the enemy was engaged.

After a few minor skirmishes and several additional attempts to negotiate with Tenskwatawa's representatives, the army continued its march over rough terrain toward Prophetstown on October 21, leaving a hundred men to guard the new stockade. Each night the column posted sentries and rose before daybreak to counter any potential Indian assault. By November 1, in cold and rainy weather, the column crossed the Vermillion River and constructed another small blockhouse, all the while shadowed by Indian scouts "lurking in the woods." By November 6, the army had arrived within a few miles of its objective on the north bank of the Wabash and prepared to attack, although the Americans were unsure of the strength of the enemy. Reinforced by sixty Kentucky volunteers, Harrison's troops advanced toward the town "very cautiously" and halted in front of their objective, a move

The U.S. Army, 1783–1811

Clouds on the Horizon, 1809–1812

that "much surprized and terrified" the Indians, who took up "positions behind a breastwork of logs which encircled the town from the bank of the Wabash," wrote a soldier of the 4th Infantry. After Harrison and one of Tenskwatawa's chiefs parleyed for a time, the governor decided to withdraw to a suitable campground for the night, anticipating a council with the Indians the next day. Several of Harrison's officers objected to this plan and called for an immediate assault upon the town, but Harrison overruled them. The army moved to "a piece of narrow rising ground, covered with heavy timber, running some length into a marshy prairie, and about three quarters of a mile north-west of the town" near the Tippecanoe River, Lieutenant Larrabee reported. The troops encamped for the night formed in a hollow square, and lit large bonfires to dry their damp uniforms and cook rations for the next day during a windy, cold, and rainy night. Wary of a surprise attack, Harrison ordered the troops to sleep with their loaded arms nearby, with cartridge boxes on, bayonets fixed, and to form a line of battle in front of their tents, in preparation for an Indian attack. The general used a single rank

◀ One of the blockhouses on the site of Historic Fort Wayne in Fort Wayne, Indiana, showing the solidity of their construction. Being a timber building, however, its greatest vulnerability was fire. (Momoneymoproblemz/CC0 1.0)

▼ This dramatic artwork depicting the battle of Tippecanoe shows General William Henry Harrison on horseback stirring his troops forward, the American ranks struggling to hold their formations in the woodland. (Library of Congress)

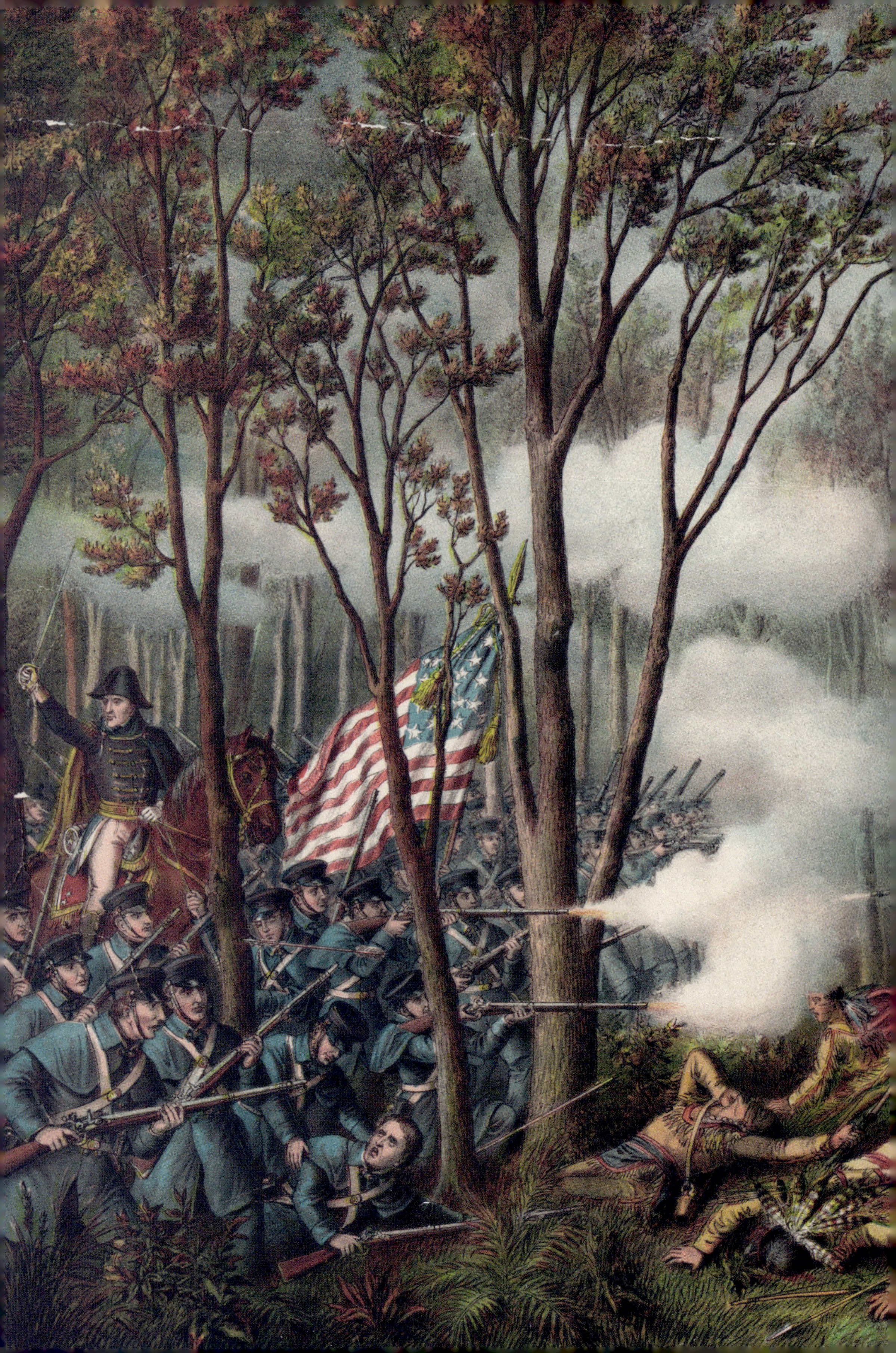

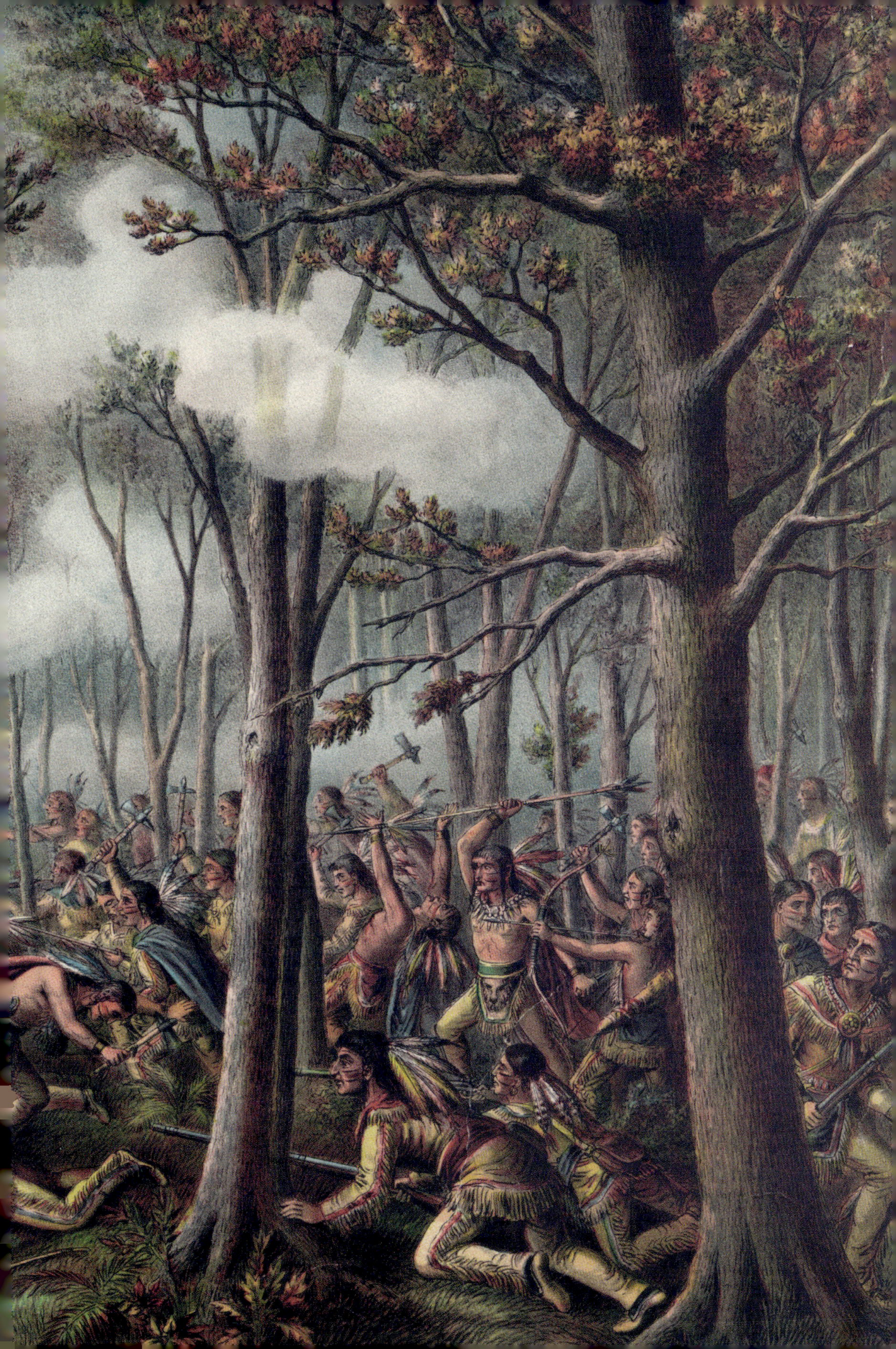

The U.S. Army, 1783–1811

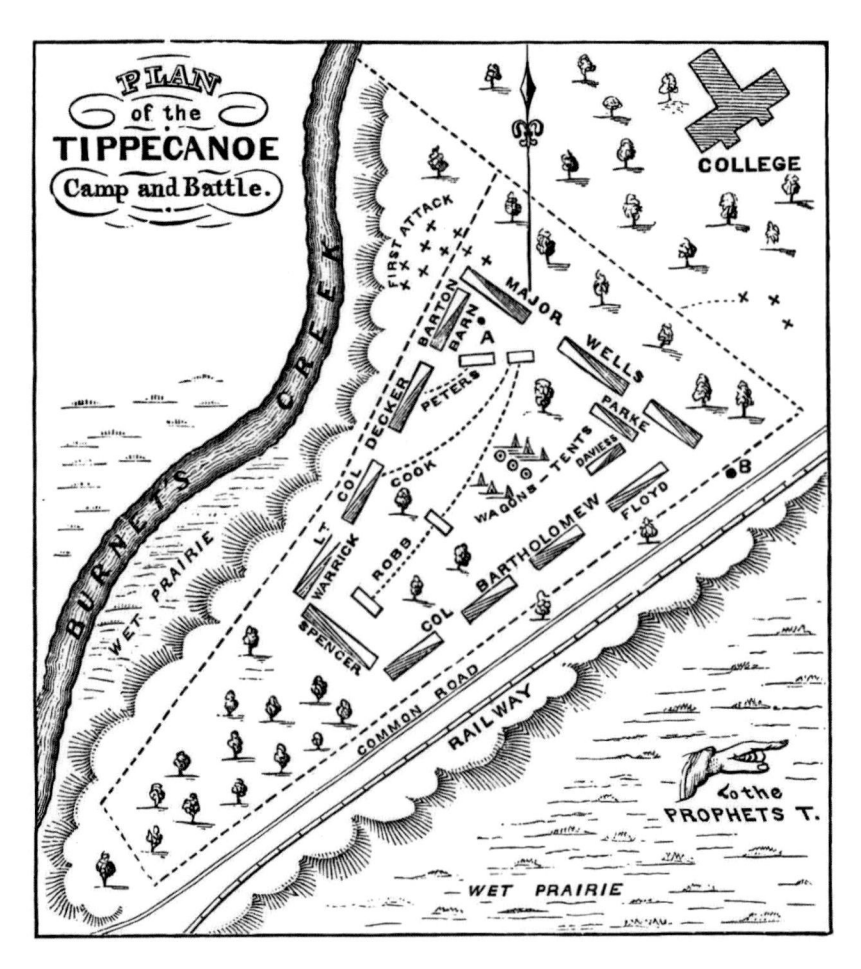

◀ Plan of the Tippecanoe camp and battle. (Ingenweb; Benson John Lossing: *Pictorial Field Book of the War of 1812* (1868))

formation "because in Indian warfare, where there is no shock to resist, one rank is nearly as good as two." The weary troops built no entrenchments or breastworks to protect the camp.

Tenskwatawa initially did not intend to attack the American camp, but some of his more aggressive warriors goaded him into action. Despite their awareness of the common Indian practice of attacking at first light, Harrison had not taken the precaution of posting extra sentries around the camp. Consequently, when the attack came at 0400, the Indians overwhelmed the pickets. As the surviving sentries rushed back to camp, the Indians pursued, yelling "like wolves, wild cats and screech owls" as they came. "Aroused by the horrid yells of the savages close upon our lines," the soldiers stumbled out of their tents into the cold rain. Some of the troops were "tardy" forming into their line and "had to contend with the enemy in the doors of their tents." In the process, the men became silhouetted against the background of their campfires, stoked to keep them warm through the chilly night. One soldier wrote that "it was truly unfortunate that these fires were not

Clouds on the Horizon, 1809–1812

extinguished the moment the troops retired to rest; for it is certain that the Indians derived a great advantage from this circumstance in the course of the action."

The "dreadful attack" first struck the company of regulars under Capt. Robert C. Barton and some of the Kentucky militia commanded by Capt. Frederick Geiger on the left wing. The sudden onslaught threw the men into disorder "before they could be formed in any regular order." The "Indians made four or five most fierce charges on our lines, yelling and screaming as they advanced, shooting balls and arrows into our ranks," recalled one soldier. The result, reported Harrison, was "monstrous carnage."

Harrison was surprised by the Indians' uncommon ferocity, but he soon restored order. The men "rallied and fought with a spirit that evinced a determination to escape the odium of cowardice," an officer recorded. Many militiamen rallied at the sight of the regulars standing their ground, despite being inexperienced in Indian warfare themselves. After a charge by dismounted Kentucky dragoons failed to dispel the Indians, Capt. Josiah Snelling of the 4th Infantry led a "desperate charge at the head of his company, with success, losing one man, who was tomahawked by a wounded Indian. The Indians fell back, and for a short time, continued the action at a distance," a soldier in the 4th Infantry observed. The troops maintained a steady fire at the warriors, who "were severely galled by the steady and well directed fire of the troops," reported a regular officer. Harrison's infantry fired cartridges of twelve buckshot, "which were admirably calculated for a night action" in which the enemy was difficult to spot. As dawn broke, the Indians made a last attempt to break the American line, but part of the 4th

▶ A 19th-century Native American bow, quiver and arrows. For much of the 19th century, a bow in trained hands was in effect superior to many contemporary firearms, have a longer range, faster rate of fire, and greater accuracy. Unlike firearms, however, it took many years of diligent practice to master the bow. (Capablancaa, CC BY-SA 4.0)

Infantry under Maj. Samuel Wells gave three cheers and launched a bayonet attack supported by a detachment of dragoons that finally put Tenskwatawa's warriors "to a precipitate flight." Harrison elected not to pursue the enemy, but instead tended to the casualties and erected a four-foot-high breastwork around the camp to deter another assault. The Indiana governor reported that "the Fourth United States Regiment, and the two small companies attached to it, were certainly the most conspicuous for undaunted valor" during the battle, and "they supported the fame of American regulars." Although some of the Indiana units performed poorly during the battle, Harrison wrote that "several of the militia companies were in no wise inferior to the regulars." He reported that thirty-eight Indians were found dead on the battlefield, while thirty-seven Americans had been killed. Twenty-five soldiers died of wounds, and one hundred twenty-six suffered nonfatal wounds. The regulars accounted for about 40 percent of the losses. Many of the soldiers' wounds were slow to heal, leading surgeons to surmise that Indian warriors had used poisoned ammunition. Additionally, some of the musket balls extracted from the soldiers' wounds appeared to have been "chewed before they were inserted into rifles for the purpose of enlarging the wound and lacerating the contiguous flesh," noted a historian.

▲ Historic marker for Prophet's Town, Prophetstown State Park, Battle Ground, Indiana. (Chris Light, CC BY-SA 4.0)

On the day after the battle, November 8, Harrison sent a detachment of mounted men to Prophetstown. The dragoons entered the town and found only an aged woman, who informed them that the Indians had left in haste immediately after the action. After loading food supplies in the army's wagons, Harrison burned the village before beginning the journey back to Vincennes the next day, low on provisions and fearful of a renewed Indian attack. Some of the troops resorted to eating horsemeat during the last few days of the march, but the troops finally reached the town by November 19. Although defeated, Tenskwatawa's Indians remained a potent threat, and by January 1812, the mystic's followers had rebuilt Prophetstown. In the spring, attacks against settlers and outposts resumed, which made the result of the battle of Tippecanoe ambiguous at best.

On the Eve of War

Even though the western frontier remained insecure, the United States declared war on Great Britain on June 18, 1812. The nation went to war over Britain's interference with American neutral trade, its impressment of American sailors, its suspected support for Indians hostile to the United States, and the affront of the *Chesapeake–Leopard* incident. Notwithstanding the measures passed in 1811 and 1812 to increase military forces, America entered the conflict largely unprepared, with an Army of just over six thousand men under arms and a Navy of only sixteen vessels. Starved of resources, held suspect by many, and more suited to the tasks of a constabulary than an army, America's military now faced once again the might of one of the world's leading powers in open warfare. The conflict, which Americans would call the War of 1812, would rage across the North American continent and the high seas until Congress ratified the Treaty of Ghent in February 1815. Along the way, America's Army would achieve some brilliant victories and endure some humiliating defeats, but in the end, the nation would emerge with its independence assured.

◀ A scene from the battle of Lake Erie, September 10, 1813, a pivotal point of the War of 1812. (U.S. Navy photo, 130906-N-ZZ999-001)

Further Reading

Coakley, Robert W. *The Role of Federal Military Forces in Domestic Disorders, 1789-1878*. Army Historical Series. Washington, D.C.: U.S. Army Center of Military History, 1988.

Crackel, Theodore J. *Mr. Jefferson's Army: Political and Social Reform of the Military Establishment, 1801-1809*. New York: New York University Press, 1987.

Kochan, James. *The United States Army 1783-1811*. Oxford: Osprey Publishing, 2001.

Kohn, Richard H. *Eagle and Sword: The Federalists and the Creation of the Military Establishment in America, 1783-1802*. New York: Free Press, 1975.

Linklater, Andro. *An Artist in Treason: The Extraordinary Double Life of General James Wilkinson*. New York: Walker & Company, 2009.

Locke, Steven P. *War Along the Wabash*. Philadelphia: Casemate Publishers, 2023.

Lytle, Richard M. *The Soldiers of America's First Army: 1791*. Lanham, MD: Scarecrow Press, 2004.

Muehlbauer, Matthew S. and David J. Ulbrich. *Ways of War: American Military History from the Colonial Era to the Twenty-First Century*. London: Routledge, 2017.

Prucha, Francis P. *Sword of the Republic: The United States Army on the Frontier, 1783-1846*. New York: Macmillan, 1968.

Stewart, David O. *American Emperor: Aaron Burr's Challenge to Jefferson's America*. New York: Simon and Schuster, 2011.

Stewart, Richard W. (ed.). *American Military History, Volume I: The United States Army And The Forging of a Nation*. Washington, D.C: U.S. Army Center of Military History, 2005.

Weigley, Russell F. *History of the United States Army*. New York: Macmillan, 1967.

Winkler, John F. *Fallen Timbers 1794: The U.S. Army's First Victory*. Oxford: Osprey Publishing, 2013.

Wooster, Robert. *The American Military Frontiers: The United States Army in the West, 1783-1900 (Histories of the American Frontier Series)*. Albuquerque, NM: University of New Mexico Press, 2012.

Index

Adams, President John 52, 53, 57
Additional Army 53
American Northwest 21, 22, 23, 25, 30, 32, 45, 46, 49
ammunition 22, 25, 34, 38, 83, 90
Armstrong, Capt. John 29–30
artillery 9, 13, 16, 28, 33, 36, 37, 53, 60, 63, 65, 70, 79

barracks 60, 63
Barton, Capt. Robert C. 89
battles
 Fallen Timbers 23, 30, 37–43, 46
 Fort Recovery 41
 Lake Erie 92
 St. Clair's Defeat 36
 Tippecanoe 23, 81, 85–91
Bayou Pierre, port of 69
blockhouses 40, 47, 48, 83, 85
Blue Jacket, Chief of the Shawnees 28, 35, 41
Boyd, Lt. Col. John Parker 83
Burr, Aaron 71–73, 75

cadets 55, 60, 61, 63
Chesapeake-Leopard Affair 73–75, 92
Chillicothe 30
Clark, Commander William 62, 64, 67
congressional inquiry 37
Constitutional Convention 18–19
construction 22, 34, 35, 38, 46, 47, 52, 53, 63,
Continental Army 9, 12, 18, 33, 39, 48, 63, 80
Cushing, Col. Thomas 69–70
customs 78

Dearborn, Senior Maj. Gen. Henry 59, 64, 67, 72, 73–74, 81

defense 13, 18, 35, 46, 48, 52, 58–59, 61, 65, 72, 75
Department of War 18, 19–20
desertion/deserters 20, 30, 34, 38, 73, 75
discipline 19, 20, 27, 30, 32, 38, 39, 52, 76
Doughty, Lt. Col. John 32

Eel River 29
Embargo Act 8
enlistment 14, 19, 55, 57
Eustis, Secretary of War William 79, 80, 83
Eventual Army 55
excise tax 44

First American Regiment 12, 13, 14, 15, 16, 25
foot regiments 53, 55
Force Bill (1809) 78
Fort Adams 40, 68
Fort Claiborne 67
Fort Clatsop 64
Fort Clinton 16
Fort Defiance 40, 43
Fort Deposit 41
Fort Greenville 38, 40, 41, 43
Fort Hamilton 23, 34, 37, 38
Fort Harrison 83
Fort Jefferson 23, 34, 35, 36–37, 38
Fort Knox 23, 24, 25
Fort Miamis 23, 38, 40–41, 42
Fort Recovery 38, 40
Fort Stoddert 65, 68, 73
Fort Washington 23, 25, 26–27, 30, 31, 32, 38
Fort Wayne 43, 81, 85
fortifications 24, 47, 63
French Navy 52

Index

Gallatin, Treasury Secretary Albert 78
garrisons/garrisoning 9, 19, 22, 25, 43, 46, 47, 52, 57, 61, 65, 67, 69, 70, 73
Geiger, Capt. Frederick 89
Great Britain 21, 22, 46, 47, 51, 62, 71, 73, 79, 80, 81, 83, 92
Greenville, Treaty of (1795) 43, 47

Hamilton, Alexander 13, 45, 52, 53, 57
Hamtramck, Maj. John F. 24, 25
Hardin, Col. John 27, 28, 29, 30–31
Harmar, Lt. Col. Josiah 12, 13, 19, 22, 32, 34, 38, 40
Harmar's Expedition (1790) 25–31
Henry, Governor Patrick 16, 19

Indiana Territory 81, 83
infantry 9, 13, 28, 41, 48, 49, 55, 56, 65, 89
insurrection 14, 19, 78

Jay, Chief Justice John 47, 52
Jay's Treaty (1795) 51
Jefferson, President Thomas 58–62, 64–65, 67, 70, 71–76, 78, 81

Kentucky militia 24, 25, 28, 34, 35, 36, 89
Knox, Maj. Gen. Henry 12, 13, 18, 20, 22, 25, 31, 32–33, 34, 37, 45

Larrabee, Lt. Charles 83, 85
Legion of the United States 37–38, 40, 42–43, 46, 48
Legionville 38
Lewis, Commander Meriwether 60, 62, 73
Lewis and Clark Expedition 61–62, 64
liquor 24, 44
Little Turtle of the Miamis 28, 29, 30, 35, 41, 43
log forts 20, 22
logistics 20, 27, 34, 38, 51
Louisiana Purchase 65

Madison, President James 79, 80
Maumee River 24, 25, 31, 38, 44
Mexico 62, 64, 67, 65, 69, 71
Miami Villages 23, 43
military college 60
Military Peace Establishment Act (1802) 58, 60

military roads 61
militia 10, 13, 14, 16, 18–19, 20, 24, 25–31, 32, 34–36, 37–38, 41, 44, 45, 55, 58, 59, 72, 74–75, 78, 79–80, 83, 89, 90
Mississippi River 61, 62, 64, 65, 73
Mississippi Territory 65, 73
Missouri River 62, 64
mutiny 11, 30

Nacogdoches 68, 69, 70
Natchez Trace 61
Natchitoches 67, 68, 69–70
National Arsenal at Springfield 16
Native American tribes
  Chippewa 21, 24, 41–2
  Creek 61
  Delaware 41
  Eel River 81–82
  Kickapoo 24
  Lenape 81
  Miami 12, 23, 24, 28, 29–30, 35, 43, 81
  Mingo 41
  Ottawa 41
  Potawatomi 41, 81
  Shawnee 24, 28, 35, 41, 82
  Teton Sioux 62
New Jersey 13, 45
New Orleans 65, 69, 70, 71, 72, 79
New York 9, 13, 78, 80
Northwest Ordinance (1787) 25
Northwest Territory 21–25, 32, 34, 37, 43

Ohio River 19, 22, 24, 25, 27, 30, 32, 34, 37, 44, 71
Ohio Territory 7

Paris, Treaty of (1783) 14, 21, 22, 52
Pennsylvania 12, 13, 22, 27, 44, 45
Piatt, Lt. William 69
Pike, Capt. Zebulon M. 64
Pinckney, Maj. Gen. Charles C. 57

Quasi-War, the 51–52, 57

recruitment 13–14, 18, 47, 55
Regular Army 45, 53, 57, 58, 79, 80
Royal Navy 46, 73

95

Sabine River 67, 69, 70
Shays' Rebellion 14, 16, 80
Snelling, Capt. Josiah 89
Society of the Cincinnati 12, 33
Spanish frontier 65, 67, 69–70
St. Clair, Maj. Gen. Arthur 25, 32, 34, 35
St. Clair's Defeat 23, 32, 34–37
standing army 10–11, 15, 18, 19, 58–59

tactics 39, 41
training 19, 27, 32, 38, 39, 58, 59, 61, 63, 74, 78
Turner, Capt. Edward D. 69

uniform 20, 44, 63, 85
U.S. Army
    1st Infantry Regiment 34, 37
    2d Infantry Regiment 34–35, 36, 37, 65, 69
    4th Infantry 83, 85, 89–90
    Corps of Artillerists 46, 48, 60, 63
    Corps of Discovery 64
    Corps of Engineers 60, 61, 63
    reorganization 37, 48–49, 58–61
U.S. Navy 57, 73, 76, 92

von Steuben, Baron Friedrich Wilhem 37, 39

Wabash River 24, 25, 35, 83
    battle of 25–30
War Department, the 18, 20, 48, 73, 74, 80
War of 1812 18, 56, 88, 92
Washington, Gen. George 9, 11, 13, 18, 22, 25, 31, 32, 33, 34, 37, 39, 45, 55, 57, 70
Wayne, Maj. Gen. Anthony 37, 38, 40, 41, 43, 45, 46, 47, 48, 49, 62
weapons
    Brown Bess musket 49
    cannon 11–12, 25, 26, 33, 36, 69
    Charleville musket 49, 56
    Harpers Ferry rifle 56
Wells, Maj. Samuel 90
West Point 9, 13, 16, 19, 33, 60–61, 63
Whiskey Rebellion 44–45
Wilkinson, Gen. James 49, 57, 59, 64, 65, 67, 69–70, 72, 73–74, 78, 79
Wilkinson, Lt. James B. 64
Wyllys, Maj. John P. 31

XYZ Affair 51–52, 53

Ziegler, Capt. David 28